IF
pews
COULD TALK

Awe-Inspiring Stories from Women of Faith

EDITED BY

Sharon Y. Riley and Jennifer M. Smith

IMPACTFUL
publishing
MURFREESBORO, TN

Published by Holy Impact Publishing, LLC
P.O. Box 11055, Murfreesboro, TN 37129

Copyright © 2022 by Agapé Perfecting Praise and Worship Center
ISBN 978-1-7353255-4-5

First paperback edition December 2022

Cover design by James McCarroll
Page layout by Soumi Goswami
Edited by Gayle "Dee" Bowman

Table of Contents

Acknowledgments

SHARON Y. RILEY

When ordinary people believe in you, great things happen. When extraordinary people believe in and walk alongside you, unprecedented things happen. One of the exceptional contributors who brought life to this project is Dr. Vincent F. A. Golphin. He is a gifted storyteller, journalist, author, publisher, and educator whose initial instruction and edits helped to illuminate the talents residing in the hearts of the contributing authors of this book. We are grateful to Dr. Golphin for the motivation and support given toward the development of *IF PEWS COULD TALK.*

Another literary gift and academician whose unwavering influence raised this project from its embryonic state is Jennifer Smith. The seed planted in her heart attracted courageous contributors who exposed their vulnerabilities and submitted to a process that will encourage countless others. Thanks to Professor Smith for her persistent and excellent spirit. Without her perseverance, these stories of intervention and courage may have merely been incubating thoughts in the minds of potential authors.

Foreword

SHARON Y. RILEY

Life is filled with challenging exposures and experiences, irrespective of your biological, emotional, or spiritual maturity. Seasons and situations are often filled with ambiguity and riddled with obscurity. Countless encounters confront your belief systems and test your faith, occasionally leaving you to question God's existence, His compassion, His abilities, and His purposes for your life. Everything that you know and believe about God may be tried at some point. God does not allow your faith to be tried with the intent to destroy it, but He allows your faith to be tried to prove that it is genuine. James 1:3 (KJV) states: *"Knowing this, that the trying of your faith worketh patience."* Out of the testing comes fortitude and patient endurance. Through the multiplicity of confidence-shaking circumstances in life, courage is renewed and trust in God's power is restored. The process may be slow and painful, but the product is authentic refined faith. First Peter 1:7 (NLT) states:

> *These trials will show that your faith is genuine. It is being tested as fire tests and purifies gold—though your faith is far more precious than mere gold. So when your faith remains strong through many trials, it will bring you much praise and glory and honor on the day when Jesus Christ is revealed to the whole world.*

You will not perish in your process. You will prevail, just like the women in this book.

This book is more than a collection of testimonies. *IF PEWS COULD TALK* is a reflective, inspirational presentation of actual triumphs and victories. Through each of them, you will come face-to-face with everyday challenges that lead you into the light of God's unconditional love. Expect your steps to be stabilized, your heart to be recalibrated, and your focus to be sharpened. Walk with these women who have faced uncertainty and intimidation. Watch for the revelation that God brings to each of them about who He is and who they are.

These inspirational experiences are shared by women who are still becoming. You will see them in the valley of vulnerability and celebrate with them on the mountaintop of victory. Before the pandemic that started in March 2020, they worshipped God from the pews almost every Sunday. They smiled, praised, clapped, and greeted their neighbors. They walked out of church encouraged and walked into staggering situations where they struggled to feel God's presence and to see God's hand at work. They are Donna Fisher, Gina Flores-Claridy, Nakia Gater, Ishné K. Hobbs, Sharon Riley, Angel

Nicole Saffold, Jennifer Smith, LaToyia Thomas, Pat Valentine, and Stormy Washington. They are more than stories from the pew. They are incredible women just like you—tried and triumphant. Their stories are real. The writers were free to share as much of their story as they chose, but some names have been changed to conceal identities. The anonymous chapters are a loose conglomeration of several women's experiences.

People on the pews are not perfect. Every day, they strive to submit their lives to God's processes to become perfected in their faith. You can begin making a similar effort, right where you are. This book is a timely and relevant tool that will help you. You will be empowered and motivated as you take this journey.

You Are Not Alone

NAKIA GATER

*The Lord is close to the brokenhearted
and saves those who are crushed in spirit.*

~Psalm 34:18 (NIV)

It was a sunny Friday afternoon. I was 20 years old, had just gotten paid, and decided to go shopping at the mall. As I sat and waited for the bus that afternoon, a small gray pickup truck broke down about 30 feet from me. I watched the driver struggle as he tried to get the ignition to crank up again. He sat there for several minutes. Nothing happened. Finally, the pickup started up again, but he did not get very far before it broke down again; this time right in front of me. I prayed because I felt sorry for him, especially because his truck was in the bus lane, and the bus would be coming soon.

After he got the engine to start one more time, the truck crawled about 25 feet. As the driver sat there helpless and persistently patient, I watched him and continued to pray. I wondered what he was going to do. I also wished someone would stop and help him. No one did. Everyone just kept driving past him like he was invisible. Suddenly, a yellow Corvette came speeding down the street and hit the small gray pickup so hard that it flew off the street and up a hill to the front door of a nearby house. I could hardly believe my eyes.

I stared in shock and then heard a loud screech that caused me to turn around. A huge black, four-door truck was swerving wildly to avoid the collision. The half-ton vehicle was headed right toward me. In a split second, I pulled my feet up onto the bus stop bench and turned my body to the side. The truck zoomed onto the sidewalk and the headlights flashed in my face. The driver managed to turn the wheel away from me, just in time. As he did, the side of his truck was within inches of my face. I leaned back as far as I could to avoid being hit. I heard tires screeching and saw nothing; it was pitch black. I thought it was the end of my life. The driver slammed on the brakes. The man quickly jumped out of the truck and stood on the sidewalk right next to the bench where I was still crouched.

"Oh my God!" he screamed. "Are you ok? Did I hit you?"

I could not say a word, so I simply nodded yes. The truck hedged me in. The driver helped me as I jumped over the back of the bench and stood next to him, trembling. He examined me and could not believe that I was not injured. We turned and looked ahead of us. The scene was haunting. The poor man in the pickup truck that was hit had been thrown from his window during the collision. He lay in the middle of the street, facedown and apparently unconscious. I had never seen anything like that before. Pedestrians and drivers rushed to him but could not revive him. People even came out of their homes. For several minutes, we all stood, watching, praying, calling 911, and waiting. Emergency assistance came after what seemed like forever. We were all deeply concerned for the man who was injured. I prayed and prayed for him. To this day, I do not know whether he lived or died.

After witnessing the horrible accident (and almost becoming a part of it), there was no way that I could just go to the mall as usual, so I walked back home. After telling my mom and grandparents what happened, I sat on my bed, speechless. I cringed at the mere thought of the condition of the poor man who was hit, but I thanked God that it was not worse because I should have been hit too. It was easy for me to praise God at that moment because of the way He spared me. There was no doubt in my mind that God loved me because of what He did for me. Knowing God and feeling God's love have always been important to me and my relationship with Him.

*   *   *

I got saved when I was 10 years old. I vividly remember the Sunday morning that I walked down the aisle of the church to the altar completely on my own after listening to my pastor share how Jesus died for me on the cross so that I could have eternal life. After I prayed the sinner's prayer, something amazing happened to me! That wonderful morning when my soul was awakened, my heart was illuminated with an awareness that changed my life forever—I was loved by the Almighty God. God kept me from getting hit that day as I witnessed the truck accident, but as the years passed, my confidence in God's love for me was shaken during times when

I was hit by life. Not by one or two events, but multiple—one right after another.

The start of those events was when a coworker and I decided to take a road trip to Georgia. We both wanted to visit family members, so we began to plan our mini adventure. As we were planning, my excitement was interrupted by a strong gut feeling, and I knew without a doubt that God was warning me not to go. I tried to back out because of my instincts, but eventually gave in to the pressure and promises of a great time. I felt that if I prayed, God would protect me from whatever He was warning me about.

We arrived safely, and I had a pleasant visit with my family, but on the night of our departure back home, the feeling returned with a vengeance. It was so strong and almost overwhelming that I called my coworker and asked if we could leave. As we got on the highway, I sat nervously in the back seat and prayed these exact words: *"God, whatever happens, please let Your angels be with us."*

A few hours later, heading south on Interstate 95 in the middle of the night, cruising and listening to music on full blast to help us stay awake, two huge deer appeared from the country darkness running full speed toward our car. We swerved all over the highway trying to avoid a collision. The deer were attracted to the headlights, so it seemed impossible to avoid them. Within seconds—and at 75 miles per hour— we hit the buck as he charged toward us. It was like hitting a running horse! We took the next exit so that we could assess the car damage and call the police and insurance company. The car was still in good enough condition to drive, so we got back on the road. I began to feel pain almost immediately, but did not think it was cause for concern, so we continued our journey. We arrived in time to make it to work right on schedule.

Within hours, while sitting at my desk, I could feel the pain worsening by the hour. Suddenly, my hand became numb, and I was no longer able to write. I called a doctor and went in for x-rays. The examination and x-rays revealed I had a cervical spine injury of several herniated discs. The intense pain caused me to take a leave of absence from work. I stayed in the bed for three full months. Due to the nature of my injury, I only found relief from the pain by lying down. Simple things such as grocery shopping, driving, housecleaning, and washing my hair had become difficult. I went to the chiropractor several times a week for therapy but did not make much progress, even after a few months. Doctors recommended that I have surgery, but I decided against it.

While adjusting to life with intermittent pain from my injury, I learned that my grandfather, my beloved Papa—the man who helped raise me and was a father to me—was very sick. Eventually, he passed, and grief smothered me on a level previously unknown to me.

Six months later, I was on my couch taking a much-needed afternoon nap when I had a startling dream. It was more like a flash—bright and intense. In the dream, I was sitting in a black car when something crashed into it. Hard. The instant the car was hit, I heard the loud sound of the impact and woke up gasping for breath. What I saw was alarming, but I knew it was God who had shown it to me. At that time, I drove a red car, so I did not feel like I was in any danger—although I did become a bit more cautious. I prayed for God's protection over myself and all my loved ones. After a while, I buried the dream in the back of my mind . . . until it came true just a few weeks later.

Nearly three years to the day of my first car accident, I was leaving work in my new, black Nissan Sentra when I was "t-boned" by an SUV. The driver of the SUV and I were both in spots where we could not see each other until it was too late. Due to heavy traffic, I relied on another driver who was motioning that it was safe for me to turn when it was not. Another vehicle hit me on the driver's side of my vehicle, slamming my head into the driver's side window and knocking me unconscious. I awakened slumped over on the passenger's side. When I was able to sit up, I noticed people banging on my windows and asking if I was okay. Disoriented, I was trying to figure out what was going on, unsure if what I was experiencing was even real. The ambulance arrived and took me to the hospital.

At the hospital, I remember the doctors telling me I had a head injury (concussion) and a bruised tailbone, but I just wanted to go home and sleep. The next day, I could barely walk because of the pain, which was getting worse. I knew soreness came with the aftereffects of a car accident, so I concluded that my feelings were normal.

It was not until over a week later when I was at home that I read my hospital paperwork in detail. I was confused by the words *"fractured pelvis."* I called the hospital thinking there had to be a mistake, but there was not. The hospital staff confirmed that I had indeed fractured my pelvis in more than one place. I could hardly believe it. No wonder I could barely walk.

Once again, I was on bed rest—trying to heal from injuries that I wished did not exist from a car accident that should never have happened with multiple injuries all at once. It bothered me that an accident that lasted just a few seconds could cause such lasting torment. I had an extremely challenging time walking. It was very slow and painful, and I could not do it for long. I could not even stand up for long without pain or sit on hard surfaces. I was in agony all the time, every day. I went from taking daily long afternoon walks to struggling just to walk to my kitchen.

After months of continued, concussive symptoms, I was diagnosed with post-concussive head syndrome because my head injury did not heal within the normal time. I had difficulties with light, sound, and motion, so it was hard to do things like driving or riding in a car, flying on airplanes, seeing bright or flashing lights, and tolerating noise, such as music or multiple conversations while in a crowd. Being unable to fly home to spend time with my family when I needed to be there was the most difficult aspect of healing from my injuries.

As my troubles started to pile up one after the other, I felt like I was in a boxing ring, getting pounded by the world's greatest boxing champion. There were so many things happening at once. *How could God bring me through all of this?* I often wondered. Trouble surrounded me. Just as I thought I was at my wit's end and could not take anything else, the worst happened—I lost my mother.

Losing Mama has been the most difficult and painful experience of my entire life, thus far. She was my best friend, my biggest supporter, my mentor, my confidante, and my sister. She was everything to me. As I write, next month will make two years since her passing. My love for her is deep—needless to say, so is my grief. Learning to live without her is extremely challenging, but I am so thankful for all the beautiful memories that we shared. Also, I am blessed to know that she still watches over me from Heaven.

The same year of Mama's passing, I also lost five other loved ones. My heart was extremely heavy. With everything

I was facing, I needed God more than ever. I felt as if I had been thrust into a dark place. I did not understand why God had allowed so much to happen to me back-to-back, especially when I prayed so hard and did my very best to live a good life. I did not realize it at the time, but I unknowingly embraced the belief that as a Christian I should be immune to suffering. If I did suffer, then I believed it was because of sin in my life for which I needed to repent. I had adopted the faulty idea that if my life was not drenched in blessings, favor, and answered prayers, then something was wrong with my walk with God. *Did I pray hard enough? Did I give enough? Did I spend enough time with God? Did I do my best to help the ones who needed me? Maybe God isn't even real. If God is real and He loves me, this wouldn't have happened*, I told myself. *All of this would have been different.*

*   *   *

Sometimes God calms the storm. Other times God lets the storm rage and calms His child.

-L. Gould

This quote is my testimony. It clearly explains how God brought me through. What I wanted and so desperately prayed for was for God to swoop in and calm every single one of my storms in an instant, in a superhero-ish kind of way. Well, that did not happen. Experience taught me that life is not always full of daisies and sunshine. Sometimes it is full of thorns and torna-does. One of the biggest life lessons I have ever learned came through a sermon my pastor preached titled "A Storm Out of Nowhere." She said, "There will be some storms in life that you will not be able to stop, but you can stock up and prepare for them." God did not stop trouble from hitting my life, but He did help me prepare for it, endure it, and make it through.

There were many times when I sat outside in the middle of the night, staring into the starry sky wondering how in the world I was going to make it until morning because of the pain I was feeling. I have stayed up until sunrise because my shattered heart would not allow me to rest. I have been so deeply terrified to the point where I could barely breathe because I felt as if the walls were closing in on me. I have lived my worst nightmare. I have paced the floor and searched for solutions that were not plain to me. I have been broken by my own decisions, the decisions of others, and situations that life catapulted at me. I have experienced pain that I never imagined possible, both physical and emotional. I know what it is to be imprisoned by restrictions that seemingly have no end. I have felt the pain of regret as the result of allowing burning rage to consume me—doing and saying things in the heat of the moment that I can never take back. Throughout all of that, I can honestly say that the only reason I am still alive today is Jesus.

My pain has been real, but so has God. Many times, when I was overwhelmed, sudden power showed up (without me even recognizing it at times), and I was able to keep moving. Strength was infused, but it was no longer mine—it was His. When I felt empty and depleted, He filled me back up again. He held me up and held me together during my darkest moments. I have experienced God breathing new life into me when I was breathless, and let me tell you, there is no feeling like it in the world! I have gone to church services wounded and weak but left empowered and full of strength and wisdom to successfully handle difficult situations. I have lost battles but won wars. I have been knocked out only to get back in the ring and be declared the champion. I have heard songs in the night that made my days easier. I have been granted much-needed grace. I have heard God's voice through scripture as the words seemingly leaped off the page exactly when I needed them. He has given me the ability to keep moving through injuries, grief, and multiple struggles so that I could make it through them.

Little by little, He brings me through. Little by little, things change. Most importantly, little by little, I change. The lessons I learned from my trials have shaped me into a better woman. I have become more aware of what truly matters. There is a beauty that comes from brokenness. My heart still aches for my mother in a way I will never be able to describe. I still suffer from chronic pain because of my injuries, which sometimes puts me right back in bed. I am still in a process of healing and restoration in several areas of my life, but through my most recent storms and the storms in my past, I have learned that God loves me when I feel it and when I doubt it. He loves me when I am flourishing and when I am suffering. He loves me when I hear Him clearly and when He is silent. God loves me on the brightest mountaintop and just the same in the darkest valley.

For Your Consideration

Life can be so difficult that we feel unloved by God. We are living out a chapter in our lives that we wish did not exist. We feel hopeless. We feel punished. Life's circumstances shake our faith. We question our worth. We may even feel betrayed by God. We cannot pray. We do not know what to do or say. We feel empty inside. Be encouraged. Life happens. It hurts. But God is real.

In the book of Acts, we read about Saul, also known as Paul. He had been a hate-filled villain, but through the power of Jesus Christ, he was transformed into a love-filled victor. Unbeknownst to him, God had a plan for Paul. God chose Paul to share the gospel of Jesus Christ and to author many of the New Testament books. Because of Paul's worship of Jesus, Paul was arrested and thrown in jail. Even there, he continued preaching about Jesus and sharing the love of God, thereby bringing transformation to several prisoners. In the book of Philippians, Paul wrote to express the joy he experienced even during his awful circumstances and to encourage believers in their walk with Christ. In Philippians 1:12-14 (NLT), Paul states:

And I want you to know, my dear brothers and sisters, that everything that has happened to me here has helped to spread the Good News. For everyone here, including the whole palace guard, knows that I am in chains because of Christ. And because of my imprisonment, most of the believers here have gained confidence and boldly speak God's message without fear.

Paul continued preaching about Jesus, not because Paul's circumstances in jail were gratifying, but because he loved God.

Sometimes, our circumstances do not reflect what we are feeling. We may be in a horrendous situation, like Paul, yet have the love of God in our hearts because we know that God loves us. Transformations from non-believers to Christians often happen in places of confinement—places where we feel constrained, unloved, and forsaken—because God dwells even amidst the ugliest places and unpleasant things in our lives. We often spend our lives searching for meaning and purpose. Paul's life reveals that living for God was his meaning and purpose. Even in bondage, Paul had a joy that could have only come from God.

But often, we may not understand our lives—why a loved one died, why we still have not had a baby, why our lives are stagnant, why we failed a state exam, why we struggle with an addiction, why our bodies were abused, why we have yet to be healed from emotional pain, or why we may be serving a prison sentence for something we did not do—but hold on as Paul did and remember that God's love for us is real. Whatever we are facing, we will get through it.

For the moment, we may not be able to see how we will escape our damnable circumstances. We cry out, "When, God, when?" We grow impatient because we cannot accept God's timing that we believe is taking too long, thus we sacrifice tranquility and joy in our lives. Disappointment sets in, and we constantly worry. We exhaust ourselves because we still have not learned to trust God. Our internal clocks are ticking, and God still has not manifested the desires of our hearts or what we believe He promised us.

We must learn to trust God and His timing. When everything in us wants to give up and question God, stay the course. Believe God. Know that He answers at precisely the right time. His Word promises us that He will not be one second late. Habakkuk 2:3 (NLT) states: "*This vision is for a future time. It describes the end, and it will be fulfilled. If it seems slow in coming, wait patiently, for it will surely take place. It will not be delayed.*

From Struggle to Strength

ANGEL NICHOLE SAFFOLD

Therefore, if any man be in Christ, he is a new creature:
old things are passed away; behold, all things are become new.

~2 Corinthians 5:17 (KJV)

Some of us struggle with some kind of addiction. Mine was sex initially, and that eventually attached itself to drugs. Ultimately, I lost my self-worth and spent most of my life trying to escape those habits. This is my story, and you will understand why I give God all the glory. He loved me. He saved me. He now calls me His own.

I grew up in the small town of Apopka, Florida, about 30 minutes outside of Orlando. There were six children in our family. From oldest to youngest are James, Lee, Aneta, Monica, me, and my baby brother Jimmy. When I was about nine or ten, my mom, Mary, and dad, Jimmy, separated. My parents allowed my siblings and me to choose with whom we wanted to live. Daddy was strict and stood firm on his rules. Mom was more laid back, and sometimes we could get away with things. So, we chose to live with her. My dad did not move far away, thus it was easy to just walk or ride our bikes to see him if we wanted. Sometimes on Saturday mornings, Daddy would pick us up to go to the flea market with him. For us, that was like going to a toy store, but we would get much more at cheaper prices.

At home, by the time we awakened for school, Mom had already left for work. James managed getting us up, fed, dressed, and off to school. But on Saturday mornings, we watched cartoons! We would wake up and race to the kitchen to open boxes of cereal. We would search for the prize in each cereal box, then get in front of the brown, wooden, floor model, color TV that had a fading screen in the right corner. I wanted to be the first in the room so that I could claim rights over the TV remote control. That way, I could watch whatever I wanted.

Plopping down on the floor one morning, I grabbed the phone and called my best friend, Tee, to see if she was up and watching our favorite cartoon. We liked the one with the all-girl rock band. I would find a shirt to put on my head and pretend to have long hair just so I could imitate the red-headed guitar player. I would stand up with my spoon in my hand, the phone tucked between my ear and shoulder, whipping my hair, popping my hips, and singing along with the introduction. Then I would fall back onto the sofa. The memory tickles me now. Tee was my best friend since we were in diapers, and she lived only minutes from me. A straight-A student, Tee was the smartest person I knew. Her grandmother, the late Ms. Ida Mae, made sure she stayed in her books. Tee made sure I stayed in mine and kept me out of trouble. Well, when she could.

Tee and I attended the church right across the street from where she lived. There was never a concern when we were at Eighth Street Church of God in Christ. On Sunday, we wore dresses that came almost down to our ankles, collars up to the neckline with a neatly tied bow that sat right at the base of our backs, and lace white socks that almost overlaid our Velcro-strapped, hard-bottom shoes. We would sing "I'm coming up on the rough side of the mountain. I'm doing my best to make it in." The pastor and elders taught us how to live the way God wants. We learned how sin separates us from God's presence.

Tee and I would leave church on Sunday afternoons, change from our church clothes, and sit on the screened-in porch at her house. We would lay on the floor to play with our dolls. After a while, we would go inside the house and play video games. As the years passed, Tee and I ended up moving farther away from each other but never so far that I could not get back to see her.

Near the end of our fifth-grade year in 1990, I started dating a boy named Rob. We were that couple who everyone thought was going to be together forever. Every morning, once we stepped off the school bus at Lovell Elementary, we would meet in the hallway with the rest of our friends and talk. He would walk me to class, give me a quick peck on the cheek, then go to his class. We wrote notes folded in the shape of hearts or stars and passed them back and forth. We were inseparable all through the summer. He introduced me to his parents. Being an only child, his parents asked a lot of questions about me, so I introduced them to my mom. Our parents seemed to get along great. His parents worked at Disney, so I was invited often. On the phone, we would talk about starting middle school. We planned to walk holding hands and all kinds of cuddly, romantic stuff. On the first day of middle school, everyone was excited to meet after what seemed like a long summer. Wearing new clothes and new shoes, everyone wanted to be seen. We were new to switching classes, so Rob and I were not able to see each other as much. Then things started to change between us. Rob told me he wanted a girlfriend who was more developed; I was flat-chested and did not have an inch of anything that was possibly growing. The other girls had matured a lot over the summer, so he broke up with me.

At that moment, rejection, low self-esteem, and fear set into my heart. *Should I let him see me cry?* I asked myself before walking away, stinging from the pain. I bottled up the hurt and pretended that I was okay. *There's nothing I can do,* I kept saying to myself. Every day, I would make sure to avoid crossing paths with him at school. Unsure of how much Rob's rejection affected me, I decided to be cautious of those I allowed into my inner circle.

As time passed, I became close friends with a girl named Angie, who was dealing with issues herself. Even though she was fully developed, she was not as pretty as the popular girls. Her hair was long, black, and curly; her skin was pale white; and she wore thick bifocal glasses. Angie was tall for her age, so a lot of people thought she was older. She lived about two streets from me, so we ended up hanging out often. She liked to walk around the neighborhood a lot, and I soon found out why. Men would whistle at her as she passed. I started liking the attention that she was getting, so I made sure that anytime I went to her house, I would have on something tight-fitting or short shorts, which back then were called "Daisy Dukes." I was about four feet, eleven inches tall and weighed maybe a buck 'o five pounds, but those men thought I was so beautiful. I wanted to be noticed. And with my recent heartbreak, I fell right into their traps.

One day, Angie told me why those men liked her so much. She admitted that she was having sex with them. I was shocked at first but intrigued at the same time. I was a virgin and afraid of even going down the road to sex. I mean . . . I was only 11 years old, but the desire to be noticed still influenced me. When the streetlights began to come on, that was my cue to go home. But when I got there, I would find myself in a daze thinking about the attention I was getting. Every day, right after school, I would go right back over to Angie's house, and we would go on our walk. Sometimes, we would stop and talk to the guys. Well, I would just stand there like a lost puppy. She would take her finger and twirl it around one of the guys' hairs. One day she whispered in my ear, "Juan said you're cute. He wants to talk to you."

Why does he want to talk to me? I wondered. I was still scarred from the breakup with Rob and feeling insecure about myself. Grabbing my hand, she pulled me toward him. We talked. Well, he talked. He told me how pretty I was and that he wanted to buy things for me to make me smile. That was a pit into which I fell head-first, and I was not trying to climb out. It felt good to be wanted. I did not know how old he was, but I knew he was old enough to drink. I went home, and all I could think about was Juan. The conversation with Angie about how she got money also popped into my head.

I did not have a desire to have sex, but I remembered what my friend Angie exposed me to and could not help but be curious. To make matters worse, I could hear almost every time my brother brought a girl home. He thought I was asleep, but I would pull my blanket up over my head and just listen. The fact that I was listening without being noticed spiked my curiosity even more. So, I started sneaking in to watch the VCR sex tapes I had found when I was at home alone. I knew it was wrong to be thinking about having sex or watching those dirty movies. I was taught in church that having sex without being married was fornication. But the exposure aroused something in me that made me set those teachings aside. I watched anyway, but I felt dirty.

Like clockwork, after school, I would go home, change out of my school clothes into play clothes, get something to eat, do my homework, get my chores out of the way, and weave my way back to Angie's house. Sometimes, I would stay around the apartment complex and hang out with my brothers and his friends. They used to jump ramps with their bikes and play marbles in the field, and I loved to do that kind of stuff, but as the day grew later, I would end up sneaking around to Angie's house. This dark side was pulling me in, and I did not know how to stop it.

One night, I went to meet Juan at his house, but I felt uncomfortable because all his friends were around, so we went off into the woods. *Oh, my goodness this is going to happen*, I said to myself as we walked deeper into the woods. He laid me down, and I experienced what I was so curious about—what it was like to have sex. Afterward, he asked, "Are you ok?" Shaking my head yes, I pulled up my pants. We started walking back toward his house, and then he reached into his pocket and gave me some money. He kissed me, and I went home. No one knew where I went or that I had money. When I arrived home, my mom punished me for being out so late, but it would not deter me from finding ways to sneak out and connect with Angie.

By seventh grade, now 12 years old, I moved again. I had finally begun developing and was "smelling myself," as the old folks would say. I started getting in trouble at school—receiving detention or suspension for skipping classes or just skipping school period. Because my mom had to work, she sent me to my dad's house.

No matter where I lived, my reckless behavior continued. This time, I met Tim, a 20-year-old, with whom I had sex regularly until his family moved out. I was lost. I did not know what to do or who to ask about where he went. Disappointed, I took a breather to collect my thoughts. I bottled up those feelings of rejection and hurt, and my self-esteem dropped—again.

As time went by, I continued acting out, now getting into trouble at home and school. The desire to be with a man became so intense that I started to have sex with random guys that lived where Tim used to live. Tim was replaced by a guy named Kevin until my daddy put his foot down. I wanted to be with Kevin so badly that I ran away to be with him. I stayed hidden for about three days. One early morning, there was a knock on the door.

"Boom, boom, boom," I heard. "Angel I know you are in there! Get out here right now!"

My heart dropped. *Oh my God, he is going to kill me*, I thought. Daddy found me. I just knew he was going to tear my butt up.

Slowly, Kevin's aunt opened the door to Kevin's bedroom. "Baby, you have to go," she said to me. Walking out with my head hanging low, I did not even look back. I just got in the car, and we drove off. That was the longest silent ride back to my daddy's house. I got a very good whipping and a long lecture about how stupid it was to do that and how much I had hurt him.

Soon after, Daddy withdrew my younger brother and me from school and picked up my eldest sister.

"You are going to Mississippi with me," he said.

I was upset, but I had nothing to say. I could feel Daddy's disappointment throughout the 11-hour drive to Lexington, Mississippi. When we arrived, we lived with Big Ma in a three-bedroom trailer. Lexington was nothing but woods and orange clay dirt roads. I was so mad, but I would not dare let my daddy see it. We lived two miles from the fork in the road, two more miles to the main road, and seven miles from *any* store. I was losing it. The houses were five miles apart. That was something I had not experienced. I was determined to get away, plotting my escape. *There are truckers who pass through every now and then,* I thought. *I am going to get a ride with one of them.*

On Monday morning, we got up and went to enroll in school. As we pulled into the parking lot, my mouth dropped. There was a huge red brick school, JJ McClain, and right beside it was a subsidized housing project. We walked in, and immediately I began to feel sick to my stomach. For one, we knew no one there. We were almost 800 miles away from our friends. The principal advised us of the rules and regulations and gave us a tour of the campus. From kindergarten to twelfth grade, the school was huge, and they believed in the paddle system for discipline. A few months in, I became friends with a girl named Jackie, who had a brother named Micky. He and I started having feelings for each other and ended up sleeping together. It was hard because we stayed almost five miles from each other. There was no way that walking was an option.

Almost two and a half years later, I had become a real challenge for my dad, and he allowed me to return to Florida to live with my mom. Since the age of 11, I had been promiscuous, and thanks to my brothers, I entered the gateway to drugs soon after my 15th birthday. My mom enrolled me in a technical school about ten minutes away from the apartments where we lived.

Now in the eighth grade, I hooked up with some old friends from the neighborhood and found my sweet spot again—men and sex. I met and slept with Terrell, who was old enough to be my daddy. That ended after my brother found out and confronted him. I moved on to Donald, a 25-year-old man who I thought took a genuine interest in me. We talked about what I wanted in life, something no one ever asked or was concerned about. That made me fall for him even more, so we ended up at his house having sex. He would call me every morning before he went to work. "Hey, wanted to see if you were up for school and hear your voice before I go in," he would say. I cuddled the phone smiling, feeling like I was on top of the world. He would come to the house while I was in school and leave me a dozen long-stemmed yellow roses so that I would see them when I got home. I knew that I was in love with him.

One morning while at school, I was walking to class and suddenly I felt sick. I stopped walking and started vomiting. School officials sent me to the nurse to lie down and called my mother to pick me up. Mom and I went to the clinic for me to get tested. It was positive. I was pregnant. My mom was so upset.

"You're too young!" she yelled. "You don't have any business messing around! I'm taking you to have an abortion!"

I was crushed. *That's not fair,* I thought. *She didn't make my sister have an abortion, and she was younger than I when she got pregnant.* Heartbroken, I just sat there crying on the inside and listening to the lecture I was receiving from Mom. She was so disappointed in me and told me that I was on my own having the baby.

"Tee, I'm pregnant, and Mom is going off," I said to my friend on the phone. She helped console me and let me know that she would be there to help whenever I needed it. Hanging up with her, I called Terrell.

"It's not mine!" he said. "I can't have more children; I got fixed."

My heart just dropped. "Ok," I said softly. I hung up the phone and paged Donald to tell him, but I did not think it could be his. He and I only slept together once. To my surprise, he was happy, even knowing about Terrell.

"Well, it's a possibility it could be mine," Donald said. I cried and told him what my mother said and how hurt I was.

"I'll be there when I get off work," he said, as we hung up the phone. He stepped up and took responsibility knowing there was a possibility that it was not his child. As always, he would call in the morning before work to check on me. I was so sick that I could not go to school. Eventually, I ended up pushing him away. I did not think he was the one for me.

At 16, most girls are having sweet sixteen celebrations; I was having a baby. My family moved again, this time to Orlando. I gave birth to a seven-pound, three-ounce baby girl named Kara. She was so beautiful. I was in love. *Now, I have someone who'll love me back,* I thought. I went back to school and enrolled her in the onsite daycare.

Life was changing, but I was not. A friend from school introduced me to her cousin Darren. Not soon after we met, I slept with him. I thought I was in love. Eventually, I moved in with him. His family fell in love with Kara. He treated her as his own. I did not want for anything. He took me back and forth to school. I stayed faithful to him. He was all mine. Well, that is what he made me think. I soon found out that he was still involved with his daughters' mother. I stayed silent and acted like I did not know and continued to stay with him. We ended up moving to Philadelphia, Mississippi. Everything was great, and Darren's Mississippi family also warmly welcomed my baby and me. However, I soon saw his true side. He abused alcohol and me.

One night, he raped me over and over until he got tired. *Lord, please help me,* I cried inside. I called my father, who lived 70 miles away.

"I'll be there soon," Daddy said.

Waiting on my dad to come, I found out that Darren was using cocaine. The ride back to Lexington with my dad was long and quiet until we reached his house. The lecture began. I knew it was coming, so I just took it. I was grateful that he came to get me, but I still did not want to stay in Mississippi. I wanted to go back to Florida, and I soon did.

Kara and I hopped on the Greyhound bus and headed back to Orlando. When I reached the bus station in Orlando, I was looking for an embrace of love or concern from my mother. Instead, I received a cold stare before she immediately turned away and led me to the car. That dug another hole in my heart. I just glossed over the hurt and kept moving.

I enrolled in school and pretended as though nothing had happened. I picked up from where I left off. I started to hang out with an old friend from Apopka named Sherrie.

"Do you want to make some money?" she asked one day while we were riding.

"Yeah, how?" I replied.

"Dancing at a bachelor party at a nightclub," Sherrie said.

"How am I gonna get in there?" I said, puzzled. "I'm too young."

"Don't worry about that," she said smiling. "Do you want to do it?"

"Sure," I said, not knowing what I was really getting myself into.

Not long after my conversation with Sherrie, we went to the club. When I walked into the club with her, everything in me tensed up. I did not know what to expect. I had never done anything like that before. I was so scared. But watching Sherrie and getting into the music, I realized that I had a sex addiction.

I never felt good about what I was doing, but somehow this demonic environment sucked me in. I loved every minute of it.

As time progressed, I lost contact with Sherrie, but I found a new connection in the club scene, watching myself dancing in the mirrors on the side walls. I started feeling like sex was my fix. Weed and liquor became aphrodisiacs that put me in the mood. Both were an instant hook. *This is perfect—men, sex, dancing, smoking, drinking, and getting paid. I'm in!* I thought. But inside, I longed to be loved and none of this satisfied that longing. Each day, I was pulled more and more into hell. I would do a show at night, come home a little after midnight, get up at 5:30 a.m., get Kara and myself dressed, and catch the bus to go to school. I hated to miss a day of school. I got good grades and tried to maintain my 3.0 GPA. My goal was to graduate.

Even though I grew up in church, what I was taught about right and wrong took a back seat once my sexual urges surfaced. I knew that what I was doing was wrong and the opposite of what the Word of God told me. Throughout high school, I continued spiraling downward, consumed by my addiction to sex, smoking, and drinking. Show after show, I would go from one man to the next—until I met Juan.

Juan pulled up in a dark blue Grand Prix with dark tinted windows. The music was so loud I stopped and watched as the window slowly rolled down.

"You want a ride?" he asked.

"Sure," I said while jumping in his car.

Juan was in a relationship, but I did not care about him having a lady. He made me feel like the only one. Even then, I still felt the need to have other men on the side. I found out that I was pregnant, but I kept going out and partying until I started to show. I gave birth to another girl two months before walking across the stage to graduate from high school. I named her Sara.

Now out of school, I needed a job. I worked at a restaurant for about two months. Even though working at the restaurant gave me a feeling of honor, I made more money dancing, so I quit the restaurant. On the way home on the bus, I met a girl named Jill. I found out that I used to be involved with her boyfriend—funny coincidence. We ended up hanging out and becoming very close. We engaged in the same reckless activities. She was about two years younger than I, but she looked older and knew more about the game. Every night, we would meet up, get our drinks and weed, then head to the club to ultimately hook up with someone for business or pleasure, depending upon how we felt.

At 18, I moved into my own apartment with Jill as my roommate. All I needed was transportation. We would have someone watch our children while we went to have sex for money. I met Erik around this time. Jill and I went to work together, and he took care of my children as though they were his own. But still, in the back of my mind, I was skeptical because of the abuse I had just experienced. Erik wanted a family, but I was too young to settle down. I was in my prime, still going to the clubs, but I stayed faithful to him. He was a good man, so I did not want to lose him. The complex where we lived evicted us because we had too many complaints from neighbors, and I soon learned that I was pregnant again.

I moved back to my mom's house. I began to feel irritated because Erik wanted to be together all the time. I pushed him away and did not want to have anything to do with him—he was way too clingy. I knew that having his baby would tie us together forever. I wanted to have an abortion.

Jill and I continued our shenanigans until we met a guy who was a pimp. He told us about a house that he had with other girls who he helped and how he could help us. We agreed to join him and his girls, so we hopped into the car. Once we pulled up to the house and walked inside, we noticed women everywhere, the youngest maybe 17. He introduced us to everyone, showed us the house, and explained more about the business. We went straight to work at 11 p.m. on Orange Blossom Trail. It is the main drag through Orange County known as "The Trail," where certain spots were popular for high volumes of prostitution and other illicit activities. Even though we were already doing this type of thing, it felt different to be working for someone else. He held us accountable, and we had to give our money to him after we finished with each man. That did not sit well with us. We were not accustomed to giving someone else our money. Beforehand, we did the work *and* kept our money. Jill and I agreed that we were going to quit, but our revelation made the pimp upset. We did not care.

A few months later, I was told that I had to deliver my baby early due to an infection in the amniotic fluid. Soon after, Brenda, two-pounds, three-ounces, was delivered by Cesarean section. That was a wake-up call. I was in shock! I had never seen a baby—my baby—in a condition like that. I was crushed. Brenda stayed in the hospital for three months. Shortly after she came home, she had to go back to the hospital where she stopped breathing. I broke down in the room when I saw my baby hooked up to all those tubes. My aunt and her pastor came to pray for her.

Somehow, I still never understood that I was in more need of prayer. I had begun to love what I was doing. It seemed natural to me. I was addicted to the high of this irresponsible, unsafe sex, always putting my children at risk. At times it felt like I was under a spell, trapped by desire. I did not stop until my longing was satisfied. I did not know it then, but sex was never going to satisfy my desire to be loved.

*   *   *

It was another century, 2001. I was still going out to clubs, dancing, and moving from one man to another, but something felt different. I started turning down opportunities to go out. I preferred to stay home. I wanted to settle down with just one man.

One day, I ran into an ex-boyfriend, Jerry. It had been almost two years, but this time, I wanted to be with him, to be a family. We tried for a while but broke up on and off. And in between those times, I turned to other men. I was still loose, reckless, and open to trying anything. One day in the bathroom at a club, my friend Jill introduced me to cocaine.

"Let me try that," I said.

"Are you sure?" Jill asked. "Stay close to me 'cause I don't know how it's gonna affect you," she said.

I did not feel any different, so I kept seeking that high that everyone else was reaching. Once I reached it, I continued doing it because that is what the crowd was doing. Now before going to the club, I wanted alcohol, weed, and cocaine. I met a man who sold every kind of drug one could imagine. I was using whatever he had. My world began to spiral even more out of control. I started popping so many pills that even they started to have little effect on me. I was left searching for that drug high that I had felt before.

A year later, I moved again but into a bigger house in Pine Hills, an urban area in Orlando. The madness continued. New places, new faces, and an old game. I would have "high" parties.

Everyone would come out to the house. We would go into a room and bring our choice of drug, and sometimes have sex. We would be up all night long. I was so empty, and I was ignoring my role as a mother to my children, but none of that mattered. I only cared about satisfying my desires. I would wake my children up, bathe them, feed them, and drive them to school. Then, I would come back home and sleep all day. I was so out of control. I craved sex like a drug addict. I started leaving my children at home to hang out with friends.

One day, while I was out, my youngest daughter, then four, was playing on the phone and called the police. When the police located me, I was handcuffed and placed in the back of a police car. I watched my children being ushered into a van. I was not even 25, and my children were taken from me. I was stunned and could not speak.

"Lord, what have I done?" I whispered.

I wanted help. I had long distanced myself from God and the church, and I knew God was the only one who could deliver me, but the devil had a stronghold on my mind. In my mind, I heard things like: *If you go to church, you know they're going to talk about you. . . . Look at the way they look at you. . . . They know what you do. . . .* I was so ashamed of what people would say to me or about me and that pushed me further away from wanting to be there.

I stayed in jail for two days and was released with a six-month probation order. As a condition of my release, I had to complete parenting classes and acquire a job. I had never in my life been arrested for anything, and I was clueless about the legal information that was told to me. I did not know where my children were for almost a month. That drove me crazy. I could not stay at home because it seemed like I could hear their voices. So, I went back to what comforted me—sex and more drugs. It was a temporary fix, but I needed to do something to ease the pain.

I began attending church with one of my friends from school, but every day without my children made me feel less and less human. I reverted to drugs. I lost so much weight that my size seven/eight clothes fell off me because I had shrunken to a size four/five. I was as low as I could be. I sat in my room with my face in my hands and cried.

"Lord, please help me," I prayed. "I can't do this. I need Your help!"

I knew there was no one in the room with me, but at that moment it felt like He wrapped His arms around me and whispered, "I'm here."

I cried myself to sleep. The next morning, I felt like a burden had been lifted. I went and applied for a job at a local store and returned home with the job. I kept attending church when I could and promised God that I would do my best to change my ways.

Soon, the state returned my children to me. I was working. I slacked off my drug use and my sexual activity, but I fell back into them both from time to time. I lost my job as a result. I was able to find another one fairly quickly, but something in my body felt strange. Instinctively, I took a pregnancy test. Sure enough, I was pregnant. *Wow!* After six years, I was starting all over again. This pregnancy kicked my butt. I had to quit my new job because I was so sick.

I left the house I rented, moved into an apartment again, and met another man, Don, with whom I began a relationship. *He has an honest job and a son, then surely, he understands responsibilities,* I thought. Everything started out great. His son loved us. My children loved him, but we both shared the same habits of sex and drugs. Eventually, he gave me a sexually transmitted disease. That caused me to deliver my baby girl Leah almost four months early, at one-pound, six-ounces. When I saw her lying in that incubator, so fragile, I just prayed and prepared myself to be there for her. *I've been through this before*, I thought. I assured myself that it was going to be all right.

Although Don and I broke up and came back together off and on, we found a house and moved, again. By this time, I had gotten so small that I could wear my ten-year-old's pants. Don and I argued so much and did drugs just as much. We fought because I did not want to be with him anymore. One night, I became so exhausted that I just gave in and agreed that we could be together. That was the only way for him to stop. I felt like I was stuck in a nightmare. No matter what I did to make him leave, he would end up coming right back. I tried to make it work. I longed for God to help me break free from the bondage I was in and from that relationship.

My cousin Ray invited me to church one Sunday. I remember speaking with the pastor's wife about my situation. I wanted to be out of the relationship without anyone being harmed. That is when she prayed with me. I believe—as a matter of fact, I know—God heard my cry. Don and I broke up without a fight. Freed from that relationship, I turned back to what brought me comfort—the arms of a man and cocaine. I would get high all night long with my next-door neighbor and return home just before the sun came up. I would slip into bed and try to get some sleep before I had to wake the children for school. I would take them to school, then sleep all day.

I wanted to do better. I enrolled in college to study information technology. I went faithfully for about two months, but once again my habits interfered with class. So, I dropped out.

In 2008, while out driving, I leaned out of my car window and yelled, "Hey!" to get the attention of a man to whom I was attracted. From that day forward, this stranger, Billy, and I quickly bonded. I became drawn to him because he did not do drugs and only drank occasionally. That caused me to hide my drug habit before eventually stopping. Our relationship reached the point that I no longer wanted to have sex with him. I wanted just to be in his presence, but I became pregnant again anyway. We moved again, but this time because the house was in rough shape. Billy and I argued and broke up, off and on.

I gave birth to another baby girl, Myra, who weighed four-pounds, five-ounces. She had to stay in the hospital for two weeks due to her weight. Billy and I began to distance ourselves from one another. I had a feeling that something was happening. We used to be all over each other, but then he no longer wanted to touch me. One day, we approached the subject of HIV and AIDS, and agreed to be tested. I got tested at my six-week checkup. My results came back negative, but he tested positive for HIV. *Lord have mercy I just had a baby with this man, and he is HIV positive.* Right then I knew God protected me.

"Lord, thank You!" I said. Many times, I knew it was nobody but God who protected me as I walked the streets late at night, climbing in and out of cars with strangers. I knew I had to change for the better.

I began attending church regularly with my cousin. No one knew my story, and I knew I needed to get my life right with God. I attended every service and went to every event. I was in love with the Word and learned so much. The pastor taught me so much, and the co-pastor, his wife, taught me how to be a woman with values. I guess because I was trying to fix my life to be right with God that the devil started to attack my children.

Kara started acting up in school and began to cut herself. That made me lean in more to God.

I remained with the church for two years, then went back to my old habits. I had learned so much and loved the Word of God, but something pulled me back to the streets. It was worse than before. I would stay out all night and leave my children at home alone, occasionally calling to check on them. I was with a guy who fed me cocaine, so that kept me going back to him. I also continued to date other men.

I still had the urge to become closer to God but was embroiled in struggles that seemed to have me bound. I connected with a pastor from North Carolina through social media. I do not remember who sent the friend request first, but we connected and conversed for a while. She invited me to join her and others on conference calls for prayer and Bible study. I was determined to press my way toward better, so I bought a notebook specifically designated for my Bible study notes. I made sure I was online. I wanted to change. I knew that I needed help. The drugs and sex made me feel like I was okay momentarily, but I knew that I was not okay.

I continued with the cocaine and alcohol, and when that urge arose to be with a man, I could not resist it. I would try to ignore the impulse by playing gospel music or reading the Bible. It worked for a couple of days, but I could not control it. I had to have it—or so I thought.

One night, I left the house to buy cigarettes, alcohol, weed, and cocaine. I was in no mood for company, so I got high at home alone around 10 or 11 p.m. A popular pastor was preaching on TV. I sat there in silence with a bottle of gin in one hand and a bag of cocaine in the other. I was so intoxicated that I could not move, but I could hear the message. I do not remember what she preached, but her words sent me into a place of worship.

I dropped to my knees and cried out to God, "Jesus, please help me. I'm so sorry!"

At that very moment, on a night in January 2011, it was like the Holy Spirit said, "No more!" I bawled. I could feel Him wrap his arms around me. I stood up, took all the drugs and alcohol, flushed them, then sat back in front of the television.

I fell on my knees again and cried, "Thank You, Jesus!" I felt like a load of pressure had been lifted off me. God heard my cry. He saved me that night.

In elation, I reached out to the pastor in North Carolina the next day and shared with her what happened. She told me that I needed a "covering." I began to tell her about a church I visited, Agapé Perfecting Praise and Worship Center, and how much I learned. I told her that I planned to join with my children that Sunday. I was somewhat afraid to return to church because of all the bad stuff I was doing. I wanted to be delivered from what was holding me. That is why I tried hard to attend church services, pray, and read the Bible. I was a single mother of five children. I thought I would be the topic of conversation. I knew I needed help. I knew that what I was doing was wrong in God's eyes. I felt convicted every time I walked into the church house. Some people welcomed me knowing what I did and that made me want to learn. Some acted like they never sinned and looked down on me, even to the point of using the Word to justify their judgment of me. They acted so saved in the church, but outside the church, those folks did some of the same dirt as me.

Something about the atmosphere at Agapé attracted me. I felt like I belonged. Sunday came, but Agapé's pastor, Pastor Sharon Riley, did not ask if anyone wanted to join. I was disappointed. I sat back in the chair. She reminded everyone of the service where she was preaching, and we followed. The following Sunday, I made sure to let someone know that I wanted to join the church. When Pastor Riley asked, "Is there anybody looking for a church home, looking to be spiritually covered?" I jumped up immediately. I grabbed my children by their hands and walked up to the front. I felt like everything that I was going through was shifting, so every time there was a service I had to be there.

After about a week or so, I found out I was pregnant once again. I was so ashamed. *Dang*, I thought. *I know I'm gonna be the talk of the church now.* Pastor Riley welcomed me and my children, flaws and all. I did not have the desire to do any drugs or drink anymore. I thank God for delivering me from that, but the urge to have sex still resided in me. I continued to see an ex-boyfriend. Every time I saw him, I felt so good at the moment. But after I would go home, I felt empty. I was being convicted. I continued to go to church, but it felt like every time Pastor Riley would teach, she was looking at me. I felt like she could see what I had done, so I kept my head down. I did not know then that it was the Holy Spirit convicting me. Hungry for the Word, I wanted to know what it took to be delivered. I kept going to service. I acknowledged that I had a problem and was ready to do anything to fix it.

I started dodging my ex-boyfriend. I knew that even talking to him made it hard for me to resist. It was even more difficult because he was the father of one of my children. As the days passed, my determination to break free from that stronghold grew. Days turned into weeks, and the weeks turned into months. I realized I was on my way. After almost two months, I had no urge or even a thought about sex.

"Lord, I know it was nobody but You who kept me," I said. I asked so many questions to Pastor Riley because I wanted to know how to stay free. "What do I need to read in the Bible?" I asked.

"Read the book of Romans and First and Second Corinthians," she said.

About six months into my pregnancy, Kara, my firstborn, started acting up in school. Almost every week, she skipped classes and got into arguments with other girls. She started to cut herself again. She began to say she wished she were dead. I knew that because the devil could not get to me, he was targeting my children. So, I continued going to church. I cried so much because it seemed as though chaos kept hitting my life.

One day, I was getting the children ready for school, and my daughter, Sara, told me that she was being molested. Everything went dark. I could hear my heart beating like the sound of a drum directly in my ears. *Lord have mercy!* It crushed me. I could not even speak. It happened right under my nose by someone that I trusted—a family friend. I kept going to church. I felt like if I did not, I would lose it.

I went to the altar and prayed. I learned how to fast, read, and study the Bible. I still struggled with the battles of Sara being molested, but my godly activities helped me stay grounded. I asked Pastor Riley every chance I could about what I should read to help me grow in my walk with Christ. I probably emailed her almost every day. Every time I needed to talk, Pastor Riley was there by email. I was afraid to talk to her face-to-face. I was hungry and had made up my mind that I would not return to the old way of life from which God delivered me. Every time there was an engagement where Pastor Riley was speaking, I was there if I could be.

I gave birth in October to a six-pound boy named Manny. I wanted a name close to the Hebrew name, Emmanuel, which means "God is with us."

I was so ready to return to church. I wanted to serve. I wanted to do something. I told myself that because I put my all into serving the devil in the world, I would now put my all into serving God and His kingdom. I joined the usher ministry at Agapé. Sister Mary was the leader. I was like a sponge and felt like I was accomplishing something. I knew that God was working in me. It had been almost two years without any drugs or sex. From then on, I knew I was the only one who could stop me. I served with all my heart because I knew if I stopped, I might slip again, and I did not want that to happen.

In the fall of 2014, my children and I were baptized. Finally, I was set free. I continued to attend every preaching engagement, volunteered at every event, and served anywhere I could. In the process, I was exposed to many different powerful men and women of God. I even had the opportunity to travel on a mission trip to Jamaica, something I never in my life thought I would ever do. I enrolled in college and graduated in July 2018 with an associate degree in medical office administration. I am proud to say that I am now the leader of the Agapé greeters, the Servant's Heart Ministry.

Writing my story brings me to tears. I am not who I used to be. I know what it means to be free. I know God is still working with me, and I stand on His promises. After eight years, I am free from drugs, alcohol, and the desire to be with a man outside of marriage. I am still trying to learn who I am because all my life I have been who others thought I should be. I have lived in fear for so long that I never thought I would ever see myself as a child of God. Today, I know that I am a child of God. I am more than a conqueror (Romans 8:37 KJV).

For Your Consideration

Drugs, alcohol, sex, pornography . . . none of these things can satisfy a person or make them feel whole, empowered, or loved. The devil wants us to believe that abusing our bodies or others is the answer to feeling alive and whole. This temporary "pleasure" often leads to permanent pain and generational curses. Only God's love was the healing balm in this remarkable story of severe brokenness, pain, low self-esteem, and rejection. But sin does not come cheaply. Often, it reverberates through our families—attacking our children and our children's children many generations down the road. When we engage in sinful lives, we open the door for various strongholds that we must fight against to save our children from being born into chaos and corruption.

It is easy to look at the lives of others and judge them. Scripture instructs: *"Do not think of yourself more highly than you ought, but rather think of yourself with sober judgment, in accordance with the faith God has distributed to each of you"* (Romans 12:3 NIV). Sometimes we believe when we are aware of another's sin that we are better than they are because they do not know our own struggles with sin. We even sometimes assign values to sin, deeming some sins greater than others. Sin is sin: *"For the wages of sin is death, but the free gift of God [that is, His remarkable, overwhelming gift of grace to believers] is eternal life in Christ Jesus our Lord"* (Romans 6:23 AMP).

God is a gracious God. No matter how many times we may need to try again and start over, He is with us through each failure. Many of God's masterpieces were deeply flawed: David was an adulterer and murderer; Abraham and Sarah were liars; Noah was a drunk; Samson was immoral; Elijah was suicidal;

the Samaritan woman was sleeping with other women's husbands, who were also in sin; Jonah ran from God; Rahab was a prostitute; and Simon Peter publicly denied Jesus. But all these individuals were given another chance, and another and another. The same is for people we know—troubled, imperfect people who overcome by the grace of God. We are not victors because of who we were; we are victors because of who we have become.

How wonderful it is that God takes us as we are and loves us anyway. How awesome it is that we can feel His presence even in our greatest despair. How beautiful it is that no matter what we have done in our lives, He still loves us. In times of our deepest despair, He is with us. Matthew 28:20 (KJV) states: *"And lo, I am with you always, even unto the end of the world."* Christ never leaves us. He is with us continually through every circumstance and tribulation.

In Christ, we are unbound by our past; in Christ, we are secure in our present; and in Christ, we have an incredible future. Addictions torment us and destroy every part of our lives and often those close to us as well. Addictions drag us to the very bottom and strip us of all hope. No addiction is capable of meeting our deepest needs, only God, as *"our sufficiency is from God"* (2 Corinthians 3:5 ASV).

As we struggle to be free from harrowing, heartbreaking and haunting situations, God loves us. We must seek the Spirit of God, who is available and desiring to help us avoid the desires of our flesh and our strong appetites for sinful behavior. It is never too late to get right with God. Galatians 5:16 (NLT) states: *"So I say, let the Holy Spirit guide your lives. Then you won't be doing what your sinful nature craves."* Reach out to God. He is waiting to receive us just as we are.

From Death to Life

DONNA FISHER

Heal me, O LORD, and I shall be healed; save me,
and I shall be saved: for thou art my praise.

~Jeremiah 17:14 (KJV)

My life took a series of turns in the last 35 years that I thought were dealbreakers. I saw myself as ruined, never to be the same again. *I just want to die*, I thought. *I give up, and I just don't care.* I am here to tell this story because God did care. He was there from the beginning.

My mother died when I was about five or six years old, so I was placed in the foster care system. As a child in elementary school, I complained repeatedly to my foster mother that my chest hurt. She would yell at me and accuse me of not wanting to attend school. When I went to school, I experienced times when I would feel my heart beating extremely fast or painfully slow. I would have to gasp for air, and then I would feel my heart beating again.

"My heart just stopped and kicked back on," I would tell any of the adults near me. But no one believed me. They would just laugh and say that if my heart had stopped, I would be dead. It got so bad that I began to believe that I was crazy. The same symptoms, and even others, were there when I attended high school. Walking to and from school, my friend Lynn would sometimes help me up off the ground. I would not know how I got there.

"It happened again, huh?" I would ask Lynn as she was helping me stand up.

"Yeah girl. You feel ok?"

"I'm really not sure. Maybe it's the heat. You know it's really hot out here."

"It is, but I'm not the one who keeps fainting," she said.

Each time, I would tell the adults when I got home, but they did nothing. No one ever inquired about how I was feeling.

The times when I would be able to go to the hospital, the staff would check my heart and say, "Young lady, you have a very strong heart. We don't see or hear anything."

I knew something was wrong, but no one believed me. So, nothing was ever done to help me.

In 1985 when I was in my twenties, the same issues began while I was working. By now, I had a son and lived with a wonderful "mother-in-love," who I called "Mom." I called her and told her I was not feeling well, but that I did not want to go back to the hospital because that did not help. I told her I would go down to First Aid, which was an office on the third floor, and that if I did not feel better, I would come home.

I went to my supervisor's office to ask if I could go downstairs to First Aid. Her back was facing me when I asked. She turned to face me.

"OMG, Donna! You look dead!" she screamed.

I felt awful, so I took the elevator from the sixth to the third floor. When I reached the First Aid office there was a sign on the door: "Out to lunch." I thought, *What?! At 8:30 a.m.?* I got back on the elevator to go to my office. By this time, I was extremely dizzy and could hardly see. Everything was blurry. I knew that when I stepped off the elevator onto the sixth floor, there would be a wall in front of me. I would need to turn to the right, and my office was the first door to the left.

The next thing I remember is waking up to voices and seeing people standing around me as I was lying on the floor in my office. I tried to stand up. Then, I saw my brand-new dress had been cut open, exposing me.

"Keep still, ma'am," said a paramedic to me.

"One, two, three, lift!" another paramedic directed as the medics placed me into an ambulance.

The next thing I heard was my mom's voice. I realized I was in the hospital. I heard my mom crying when she came into my room. I saw a doctor standing over me.

"You have a rare type of rapidly growing tumor," Dr. Jackson said. It's pretty serious, and I am not sure how you have survived this long. The tumor is impacting your heart very seriously. Your heart stopped beating a few times it seems, according to the medic report, but it was revived with CPR. My team will remove the tumor by cutting a half inch under your armpit."

I heard my mom's sniffles through her tears. I was just relieved she was there for me.

"Will I be all right?" I asked hopefully and lifting my hands up in the praying position for Dr. Jackson to see.

"We sure hope so," he responded with a smile.

The hospital flew a surgeon in who had previously performed the sophisticated type of procedure that I needed. After surgery, I awakened to lots of small chatter in the background. I opened my eyes and saw that I was surrounded by my family, Dr. Jackson, and the surgeon.

"You, young lady, are lucky to be alive," Dr. Jackson said. "Your heart stopped beating again on the operating table, but we made it through."

I tried to respond but could not. Somewhere along the way, something happened during surgery—I could no longer talk. Slowly, I made a motion to indicate I needed paper and pencil. A nurse handed me her pen and a piece of paper. I scribbled: "What's going on? I can't talk. Am I okay?"

Dr. Jackson warmly chuckled and said," You made it through," and squeezed my hand, "but you will have to learn how to talk and walk again."

Over the next few weeks, I succeeded at both. It was hard, but I did it! Praise God!

One morning, I got out of the wheelchair and walked down the corridor singing "Amazing Grace." Though my stitches and staples still needed to be removed, I knew I could go home soon. I was so relieved because I had been in the hospital for a long time. A few days later, I was leaning over on the side of the bed for the removal of the stitches and staples. When Dr. Jackson finished, the nurse told me to stand to see how I felt. BOOM! Down to the floor, I went.

"Whoa! Help her up please," Dr. Jackson said. "The staple must have hit a nerve or something. Let's get her up and back in the bed."

The medical team gathered around me to help me back in the bed. I assumed I would be okay, but I had to learn to walk all over again. I was upset—no, I was mad that this was happening to me. I was tired and wanted to feel healthy. After learning how to walk again, I was finally released after almost three months of being hospitalized. *To God be the glory!!* I thought.

Looking back, I can clearly see that God was with me the entire time, even when I doubted Him. And the times that I fainted I was unable to pray for myself, but someone was praying for me. At one point, I was even angry with God and was tempted to give up. Fear gripped my mind, heart, and soul, but I persevered.

For almost twenty years, I generally felt okay with some random days when I would collapse. I stopped telling people because it seemed like no one believed me. Lynn and I would laugh because neither of us knew what was happening, but she also knew that no one believed me. To others, I would pretend that I accidentally tripped, but Lynn and I knew that something was not right.

Then in 2004, the day after Hurricane Charley, I woke to paramedics talking to my daughter, extended family, and me. My daughter said I suddenly stood up and said, "Uh-oh, here it goes again," before dropping to the floor at the hospital.

"Donna, Donna... Can you hear me?" the nurse said.

I heard the nurse and someone crying. I opened my eyes and saw the nurse and my daughter, who was crying. My chest was hurting badly. I had a headache and pain all over. I found out later that as the doctor was walking out of my room to check my test results, "code blue" was called. The EKG monitor indicated that my heart had stopped again, but the nurse hooked me up to the defibrillator machine. My heart pumped on by the mercy of God!

The doctors informed me that I would need a pacemaker-defibrillator implanted in my chest. I consented to the surgery, hopeful that my years of discomfort would come to an end. For the most part, the device worked well for over a decade.

Then, on December 22, 2017, the defibrillator, which sends a shock to the heart to restore the normal heartbeat, fired. I was sitting at the dining room table having a tea party with my grandchildren. The next thing I remember was someone calling my name.

"Mom . . . Mom . . . Mo—," said my daughter while shaking me. I could hear my eight-year-old granddaughter crying loudly.

Not realizing I was on the floor, I asked her, "Why are you shaking me?" I thought I was still sitting at the table.

Helping me to the couch, she responded, "I think you fainted, Mom."

My granddaughter told me that while I was sitting at the table, my eyes suddenly rolled back in my head before I fell out of the chair and hit my head on the concrete floor. I instructed my daughter to take me to the hospital because something was definitely wrong.

When we reached the hospital, a technician came and hooked me up to a monitor. He advised me that apparently it all happened so suddenly that my pacemaker did not have time to adjust my heart rate. By the time I hit the ground, I had no heartbeat, so the defibrillator sent a hard shock to jumpstart my heart.

"Oh my God . . . oh my God!!" the technician yelled while looking at the monitor reading.

"What's wrong?" I asked.

"This is really unbelievable. I need the doctor to come and look at this now!" he told the nurse, who then ran out of the room. He turned to my daughter and said, "Your mom has a guardian angel watching her and praying for her. Someone must really like her. Her heart rate sped up from 0 to 350 bpm in half a second! That's incredible!"

The medical team came and handled everything. Eventually, I was released to go home.

I am so grateful for the doctors who implanted the device in my chest and sewed the wires into my heart. However, if it had not been for the Lord God Almighty, who blew the breath of life into me after the device shocked me, I would not be sitting at the same dining room table writing my story now. From that hospital bed to this day, I continue to sing the song "Great is Thy Faithfulness" in my head and from my mouth. The part of the song that stands out to me is: "Morning by morning, new mercies I see. All I have needed thy hand hath provided. Great is Thy faithfulness, Lord unto me!"

For Your Consideration

Many times, the situations from which God pulls us are so unbelievable that we know they had to be God. We know that nothing we could have done would have resolved the issues. Often, someone was praying for us at times we were unable to pray for ourselves. People often casually ask us to pray for them. Our response is usually just as casual, "Sure." And we will if we remember to do so in our prayer times. But we often forget. We forget because we do not see other people's problems as our issues. So, we intend to pray, but it is just not our problem, and we have our own issues. When someone asks us to pray for them, we should do it right away. Saying a prayer can be quick, silent, and still effective. God hears the prayers of those who intercede for us. Sometimes we cannot pray for ourselves, but God honors the prayers of others just as He honored Elijah's prayer for the widow's son.

In 1 Kings 17, a widow's son died. She went to Elijah the prophet, who was staying at her home in the upper room, and told him that he allowed her son to die and questioned why Elijah would do such a thing. Elijah brought her son to the upper room and began questioning God as to why He allowed the son to die. Then, Elijah laid his body on the son and prayed: *"O Lord my God, I pray thee, let this child's soul come into him again"* (1 Kings 17:21 KJV). The Lord heard Elijah, and the son was revived and lived.

When God places people on our hearts or minds, we must pray for them. We may be the ones sent by God to intercede. They may even be in a situation where they cannot pray for themselves. Never underestimate how God can use us to intervene in the trials of others. He will hear our prayers for others. He will honor our sincerity in caring about others. He will reward our obedience in praying for others. This will help us to develop spiritually. We should be generous with our prayers and pray for others always.

Prayer is particularly powerful in times of crises. Matthew 18:18-20 (NIV) states:

> *Truly, I say to you, whatever you bind on earth shall be bound in heaven, and whatever you loose on earth shall be loosed in heaven. Again I say to you, if two of you agree on earth about*

anything they ask, it will be done for them by my Father in heaven. For where two or three are gathered in my name, there am I among them.

Prayer is more than just talking with God; it is a form of worshipping God that fortifies our need for Him. It is our chief weapon against the enemy that brings the power of Heaven down to earth. The Bible instructs *"always pray and never give up"* (Luke 18:1 NLT). There are no magic words to pray—pray with humility and a receptive heart to our loving God. He promises to hear and answer: *"The righteous cry out, and the Lord hears them; he delivers them from all their troubles"* (Psalm 34:17 NIV).

The Path to the Light

LATOYIA THOMAS

*Behold, I am the Lord, the God of all flesh:
is there any thing too hard for me?*

~Jeremiah 32:27 (KJV)

As I stare at a black and white photograph, my eyes begin to well with tears. The salty drops moisten my lips. A knot forms in my throat and silences me like a stern "hush" from my mother. Anger covers me with wicked serenity. Confusion, hurt, and helplessness open a time capsule to the worst season of my life.

Three months before that picture was taken, my mother, Grace, noticed that my three-year-old daughter, Maleah, appeared to have swollen glands. Mom insisted that I take her to the doctor. She thought that it might be an infection. The doctor placed my daughter on antibiotics. Just a few days later, Maleah's glands enlarged even more. It was a weekend, so I took her to the hospital. The on-call physician ordered a battery of tests, one of which showed that Maleah's white blood cell count was higher than it should be. I was given the rundown of possible ailments that could cause the spike in her counts. She was tested for many of them—meningitis and influenza, among other infections—all of which were negative. We were sent home with instructions to follow up with her primary care physician and continue the antibiotics.

That Monday, while on break at work, I called the doctor and informed her of the weekend's events. She responded that she intended to send Maleah for blood work later in the week but urged me to take her to another hospital right away. I told my boss that I had to leave, and she obliged. *Awesome, I get to leave work early*! I thought. I did not have a care in the world. As I arrived at my mom's house to pick my daughter up, I joked, "Hey, Love Bug! We have to go to the hospital to find out why you look like a blowfish!" I can still hear her infectious laugh. Maleah laughed as if she knew the importance of the business of laughter. After she gave my mom a hug and a kiss, we were off.

*   *   *

"Thomas, Maleah? Thomas, Ma . . . ," called the nurse.

I jumped up and waved my hand, "Here we are!" I said and scooped up my daughter and purse. "So, what brings you guys in today?" the intake nurse asked, as she dotted Is and crossed Ts on forms.

"Well, about a week and a half to two weeks ago, we noticed that her glands were swollen," I said while pointing at Maleah's throat. "I took her to her doctor and was given antibiotics, but they just got bigger! Saturday, I took her to a hospital and was told that her white blood cell counts were high. She was tested for the flu and meningitis, and some other infections, but the tests were all negative," I said, somewhat unsure of the accuracy of what I was saying.

"Ok, did she start a fever—or—what made you come in today?" the nurse questioned.

I told her that Maleah's primary doctor sent us over after finding out about the hospital visit over the weekend. After taking her vital signs, temperature, and weight, we were sent to a room in the back to await another doctor, the staff physician. This doctor informed me that he reviewed the charts from the other hospital.

"Some of these tests help determine what is wrong, but some are pointless," he said with an annoyed tone, "a-a-and the ones that are most important weren't done!"

After apologizing for the frustration that he displayed over what took place at the other hospital, the doctor advised me that he would order blood work and more tests. Not long after the blood was drawn, he returned. This time he seemed to fight with himself. He stood at the door for a moment, shoulders slumped, eyes lowered. Obviously, he was the bearer of bad news. He knew he had to do it, yet he would have preferred not to. The doctor began by explaining the function of the white and red blood cells. He then told me that Maleah's white blood cell count had more than doubled since our hospital visit on Saturday.

"Although I can't say with 100 percent certainty, it seems that she may have leukemia," he said somberly. "Further tests will need to be done to confirm, but with the dramatic spike in her white cell counts, it is a very high indication of leukemia."

"Wa—wait a minute, LEUKEMIA?!?!" I said louder than intended. "That's like cancer or something, right?" My breathing increased. "No, uh-uh, she doesn't have that! You have to do your test again because you are wrong!"

"We are going to admit her to run more tests," the doctor said in a manner that sounded robotic. "I am very sorry. I wish you both good luck."

Within minutes an orderly arrived to take us to a room upstairs. In a whirlwind of purposeful chaos, she got instructions from the ER, grabbed our paperwork and belongings, and ushered us to the elevator. "Going up," she said. The doors closed on life as we knew it.

*   *   *

I remember the sound of IV pumps beeping, codes being announced over the loudspeaker, and hearing the heavyset Black lady with short salt and pepper hair answering a call from one of the rooms, "Yes, okay. I will let your nurse know." I recall cheerful hellos from nurses whose eyes seemed to say they wished they did not have to see the faces they served. Not because they were tired or hated their jobs, but because their souls ached. Their hearts began to cry whenever they got a new patient on the seventh floor. The orderly showed us to our room in the Hematology/Oncology unit, then wished us good luck as she walked away.

I sat down on the bed and held Maleah tightly as I tried to understand what was happening. My mind raced but was not forming any clear thoughts. The staff physician's words replayed in my head like a scratched record. I could not make them stop.

It seemed as if I was outside of myself watching events unfold. There was a light tap on the door. Within minutes, a team of doctors, nurses, and other hospital staff entered the room. Jessica, who I learned was the oncology team's nurse, walked in first. Her wide smile desperately, yet unsuccessfully, attempted to brighten the darkness that engulfed the room.

In a Southern accent with a tone that displayed complete confidence in her words, Jessica told me she would assist with Maleah's treatment. The woman assured me that she was there if I needed anything. All I could think was, *Jesus, why do we have an oncology team?!*

A nurse practitioner, Becky, was next. She held files and papers close to her chest as she leaned forward to shake my hand. Her shoulder-length blonde hair was pushed behind her right ear, which is also where she stored her ink pen. With a serious face, she explained that she would provide me with paperwork and information about Maleah's diagnosis and treatment plan. Becky would be available to answer any questions.

When the team doctor walked into the room his cheerful spirit preceded him. He was a thin man of average stature with short brownish hair, thin-rimmed glasses, and Disney characters emblazoned on his necktie. He assured me that they would do everything possible for Maleah. More than that, he was confident in the treatment plan they had developed for her. He connected with Maleah immediately, making silly jokes and funny faces at her while the others talked to me.

Another doctor was a silver-haired man with hopeful, sad, and determined eyes. His forehead wrinkled with the weariness of interacting with countless families who had been in our position. His concern and love were sincere. I could tell he was in charge before he uttered a word. But when he did speak, the words seemed foreign and incomprehensible.

"Your daughter has acute lymphoblastic leukemia with a B-cell precursor," he said firmly.

Though he spoke humbly and with compassion, those words were harsh and rough. He may as well have cursed me out! I was offended that he had the audacity—no, the NERVE—to walk up in my face and tell me about *my* child. *I don't know who he thinks he is talking to, but this news is not for me!* I thought. *This man must really not know who he is talking to. He is one brave somebody to walk in the room and make such a bold statement . . . to me!! Hadn't he heard about me? Didn't he know that you don't mess with my family, especially not my children?*

"No suga, uh-uh, naw," I said, shaking my head with my hand on my hip. "You have those results mixed up with some-one else's. You can't speak that over *my* baby. Don't you know there is power in your words?" My face was like stone, my heart a bass drum pounding relentlessly. My entire body trem-bled uncontrollably. "You are in the wrong room!" I insisted pointing at the folder he held. "You better go tell that to some-body else, or you need to have them redo her tests because that . . . that is not right! *That* is not for us!"

"Mrs. Thomas," he said. "We have tested and retested. The results have been looked at by . . ." I could not hear him. I had no idea what he said. His mouth moved, but there were no words. No words.

When I could hear again, he was saying, "Mrs. Thomas, Maleah has b-cell precursor acute lymphoblastic leukemia, which is very aggressive, and she needs to begin chemother-apy right away. We have scheduled her for surgery tomorrow morning to have a central line placed. She will be given the chemotherapy drugs through the line. We would like to start treatment as soon as possible."

I could not breathe. I felt like I was dying.

"I told you to retest her!" I insisted, sobbing and holding Maleah as tightly as I could. "I am not letting you operate on my baby! I'm not going to let you give her chemotherapy. Your tests are wrong! How will you feel knowing that you've done surgery and given chemo to a child that has nothing wrong with her?" I yelled between sniffles. "I just will not let you do it because I refuse to believe that this is true! God wouldn't allow this to happen to her. . . . He wouldn't allow it. There is no reason for her to have to go through this. She is only three— she's just a baby! No, this is wrong, God wouldn't do this to her. I refuse to . . ." I sat down on the bed with tears streaming down my face. I just cried and rocked. Between gulps of air I mumbled, "I don't think God . . . God wouldn't let this happen to her."

"Mrs. Thomas, I am a Christian as well, and sometimes God heals us by using medicine," said Gina, the pharmacist, who sat next to me and held my hand. "I think you should allow us to treat Maleah. The test results are correct, and now it's time to think about treating her."

My mind and heart raced. Gina gently squeezed my left hand. I could not form a thought. I could not believe what those people were saying to me. I told them I would need to think about it. I needed to pray. I needed to call my husband and mom.

"Ma, they say she has leukemia," I cried.

"What?! Toyia! What did you say?" Ma yelled into the phone.

"They said she has leukemia. They want to operate and start chemo tomorrow! I told them no!" I said still crying, but a little more audible. "I told them they had the results wrong."

My mother was silent for a moment.

"I think . . . maybe . . . you need to let them do it," she said just above a whisper. I could hear the pain in her voice, but she did not cry on the phone. My heart broke.

"Ma, what if it's wrong?" I asked in tears. "I don't believe it, because God wouldn't do this," I cried.

"Toyia, God can still heal her," Mom said. "He has a plan, but maybe this is how He is going to heal her. We still trust and believe that He can and will work miracles for her, but you need to call them and tell them to start the treatment."

What is going on? I thought. *As soon as I decided to dedicate my life back to God, He allows this to happen. I can't believe He would do this. What did Maleah do to deserve this? This happens to other people, the ones on talk shows and made-for-TV movies. This doesn't happen to run-of-the-mill, regular folks.*

I felt helpless and defeated. I felt betrayed by God. *Why my daughter?* I wondered. This whole thing was senseless. For as long as I can remember, I have been a protector. Even as a little girl, I instinctively protected my family. Ask the boy who pushed my cousin Todd down on the school bus; ask him what I did to him. Ask the kid who teased him outside of my fifth-grade classroom. Ask the girls who tried to jump my niece. If I know about it, I'm going to handle it because you do not mess with the people I love. But not this time. I was down for the count. I could not defend or protect my baby girl. *What kind of mother am I?* I wondered. *What was I good for at that point?*

Although, as I look back, I can see God's hand in this. I was mad. Like the writer in Psalm 22:1-2 (NLT), I wanted to cry: "*My God, my God, why have you abandoned me? Why are you so far away when I groan for help? Every day I call to you, my God, but you do not answer. Every night I lift my voice, but I find no relief.*"

I pretended to be on good terms with God, but I had fallen out with Him. I talked about Him. I asked people to pray and fast. But I was not feeling Him right after the diagnosis. He betrayed my daughter. You do not mess with the people I love. I could not talk to Him. Every time I tried, I thought about how He let this happen to an innocent baby. I never stopped believing in Him or His power, I was just so confused and angry with Him that I could not bring myself to talk to Him for myself. I was thankful for the prayers of my family and friends in those first few weeks because my heart and mouth were closed.

The morning after the diagnosis, my husband, son, mom, and nephew came out to the hospital for Maleah's surgery. The surgeon and anesthesiologist came in to brief my family on the surgery. They explained that they would be placing an external IV port in her chest to administer chemotherapy and other IV medications and to also draw blood. The doctors told us that it was a simple surgery that would take approximately an hour. To me, there was nothing simple about any of this.

I held Maleah while we sat in the pre-op room. My husband, mother, and I showered Maleah with kisses as they wheeled her away. As soon as they were out of sight, I broke down. I cried until my throat and head hurt and the tears stopped coming. I cried until there was no sound. Then, I cried silently. After a while, I pulled it together enough to go out to the waiting room with the rest of my family. We sat and waited. I paced and watched the clock. Waited. Paced. Watched the clock. Finally, time was up. But no one came through the door. *Where are they?* I thought. I went and stood at the reception desk, but the receptionist just sat there. *Ok, she's busy,* I said to myself. *I'll just wait.* Another few minutes passed. The woman at the desk still had not offered any assistance. She picked up the phone and hung up the phone. Walked away and came back. Still nothing.

"Am I invisible or don't you see me standing here?" I asked. "I've been standing and waiting, but you have yet to acknowledge me. What is the problem?"

"Oh, ma'am, I am so sorry. I didn't realize you needed help!" she explained.

"You thought I was just standing here at your desk for fun?" I asked. "Whatever! . . . They said my daughter should be out of surgery by now, but I haven't heard anything." Nothing about my interaction was Christ-like. She requested my name and my child's name and promised to return with Maleah's status. After a few minutes, she told me that someone would be right out.

"Mr. and Mrs. Thomas?" a voice called out. We stood. The doctor walked over to us. He told us that the surgery went well. Maleah did well. She would be in recovery for about 45 minutes, and then an orderly would take her back to her room. The doctor warned that she would be sore and in pain. He told me to make sure that she takes it easy. We obliged, thanked him, and hurriedly left the waiting room.

When they wheeled Maleah's bed back into her room, she was wide-eyed and ready to start her day. She wanted to play with her brother and cousin. I tried to stop her, but she insisted that she was fine. She led her two playmates out of the room to find an adventure. When the lead doctor and his team came into the room to check on Maleah not long after she left to play, they thought she was in the restroom. They were astonished when they found out that she was in the playroom. With a bewildered smile on his face, he said, "That is remarkable." They outlined her treatment plan and schedule and told us what to expect.

She would be on chemotherapy for two years. First, there would be in-patient cycles where we would check into the hospital for a week twice a month, followed by weekly outpatient chemo infusions. Maintenance would be a combination of out-patient treatments along with a regimen of chemo and steroid pills. After explaining the plan to my family and me, the doctor went to the playroom to look at Maleah's port because she was too busy to come back into the room. When he returned to us, he reiterated his astonishment about how quickly she was up and active after the surgery.

The doctor's amazement continued throughout Maleah's treatment. On more occasions than I can count, all her doctors admitted to being baffled by her progress, response to treatment, and overall ability to bounce back, considering what she was being exposed to. Chemotherapy is literally poison. It is, however, the lesser of the two evils. We were blessed. Maleah did not suffer from many of the side effects that are associated with chemotherapy. Other than a brief bout with mouth sores, weight loss, and some skin and nail discoloration, she breezed through the entire ordeal. Many cancer patients do not have that testimony.

There was one side effect for which I must admit I was ill-prepared. She was on treatment for about a month with no hair loss, so I convinced myself that she had odd, defying hair that simply would not fall out. Maleah is a girly girl, who at two years old, refused to take a family picture without putting on a fresh coat of lip gloss. So, it is understandable that my heart packed up its belongings and took up residence in my stomach when I noticed that her braids were beginning to peel up around her hairline. It was no surprise that breathing became as foreign to me as Istanbul when I further discovered that she was completely bald underneath her ponytail. The only things securing her long, thick, beautiful locks to her precious head were a few reluctant, defiant strands of hair.

I motioned to my mom to come take a look. She grabbed my daughter and held her as if she were transferring all the love inside of her through that hug. I cried in the bathroom. Maleah was just a baby. The three-year-old did not deserve that. After collecting myself, I explained to Maleah that her hair was falling out from the chemotherapy. I told her that only a few strands of hair were still attached to her head. I assured her that the hair would grow back longer, thicker, and prettier than before. I asked the permission of my three-year-old daughter to cut her braids off. She acquiesced, and then she was bald. As she scurried off to the full-length mirror in my mom's room, grace quietly summoned Jesus. Maleah walked back into the living room. We sat, mouths agape.

"Mommy, I have a cute head!" she exclaimed, with one hand on her hip, one leg cocked out in front of her, and rubbed her baldness with the other hand. The room erupted. We laughed and cried. My heart started the long journey back to its own home. At that moment, I knew we would get through. We were going to be just fine. Her strength gave me strength. She was in the middle of a fight for her life and had just lost all her hair, but she only saw the good. That simple statement, her resilience in the face of adversity, taught me so much about where I wanted to be spiritually.

I was having a crisis of faith. I knew God was there . . . somewhere. I decided not to chase after some God who I felt abandoned me when I needed Him most. I was wallowing in fear and frustration. I was throwing a tantrum. Maleah, by God's divine appointment, was an example of how to respond to life's trials. I had not had a real conversation with God in weeks, but that immediate reaction from a toddler who had just experienced the trauma of going bald reminded me that God is still God, regardless of what it looks like.

Now, I look at this black and white photograph. I see my daughter—my baby—standing tall and proud, and looking straight into God's eyes. Around her neck is the toy gold and ruby necklace given to her by our pastor. When Maleah was in the hospital, they had an impromptu tea party. In this black and white photograph, she wore a pink skirt with embroidered flowers at the bottom. Her hospital ID bracelet was a mandatory part of the ensemble. IV lines, or "tubies," as the patients and nurses called them, conspicuously bulged under her white shirt with the tiny pink bow at the neckline. IV lines are lying on the floor, trying desperately to hide from the camera, and in the distance, beyond the scope of the lens, an IV pump with a fully charged battery is steadily pumping various drugs into her bloodstream by way of the catheter that was surgically implanted in her chest months earlier. Maleah's lips are pursed. Her eyes are deliberate. Everything about her says courage, confidence, and determination. In all the darkness that surrounds her, she is the persistent light that shines through. Thinking back on this season reminds me of so much pain, helplessness, and uncertainty, but it also reminds me of strength, hope, faith, and love.

More than 11 years later, everything chemotherapy took away from her has been replenished. Maleah has had no long-term side effects from her treatments. She excels in school. Her prayer that God would give her back her hair was answered. Maleah was healed by the Blood of Christ this I know for sure. Isaiah 53:5 (KJV) states: *"But he was wounded for our transgressions, he was bruised for our iniquities: the chastisement of our peace was upon him; and with his stripes we are healed."* When I flip through our family pictures, none of them makes this passage of scripture more real or relevant than the photograph of that little girl with the infectious laugh and unbreakable spirit. It reminds me of the time we fought leukemia and won.

I know with certainty that whatever we are given to bear, we are also given the grace to handle it. I became acquainted with my own strength during that time. My faith and my sanity were tested. I am ever so thankful to God. God's hand and plan are the only explanation for the favor that we experienced. This was one of the hardest things I have ever had to walk through. It made me realize that *"with God all things are possible"* (Matthew 19:26 NIV).

For Your Consideration

When a child is sick, we wonder what sins were committed that cursed a little baby. But a story in the book of John reveals God's greatness. John 9: 1-3 (ESV) states:

> *As he passed by, he saw a man blind from birth. And his disciples asked him, "Rabbi, who sinned, this man or his parents, that he was born blind?" Jesus answered, "It was not that this man sinned, or his parents, but that the works of God might be displayed in him.*

Here, there was a man blind from birth. He was not blind because of his nor his parents' sins, but so that God's good works would be revealed through him. Jesus healed the man, and his sight was restored. All who knew the blind man as a beggar questioned this healing and the Healer. This story reveals the miraculous, healing power of God.

Our grief about our illness or the illness of a loved one can be crippling, so much so that we depart from our routine prayer life. We may decide not to fast. We may ignore Jesus but pretend like we are leaning on Him for healing and strength. We may go through the motions in prayer but not really believe that God will heal because we do not even understand why our loved one is so ill in the first place. We look for people to blame. We look for a purpose for the pain that we feel and that we see our loved ones experiencing. We blame ourselves for our lifestyles, generational curses, and other things that may contribute to trials that we face.

During trying times, we focus on God. Even when we feel we cannot pray, we focus on what we would say to Him if we could say anything. We think about what we really want to say to Him if we had the courage to express our anger with Him. Ultimately, trials develop our endurance and perseverance, which help us to trust in God. Trials reveal our weakness and our great need for God. Trials shine a light on where we can grow in our spirituality and help us understand God better. Trials lead us into greater worship and to become better witnesses for God. Second Corinthians 1:3-5 (NIV) states:

> *Praise be to the God and Father of our Lord Jesus Christ, the Father of compassion and the God of all comfort, who comforts*

us in all our troubles, so that we can comfort those in any trouble with the comfort we ourselves receive from God. For just as we share abundantly in the sufferings of Christ, so also our comfort abounds through Christ.

God comforts us as we comfort others. Often, we minister out of our misery and the consolation received by God during our sufferings.

Rarely do we think that perhaps a trial is to reveal the greatness of God. But this was the case for the healing of the blind man and Maleah. Their infirmities were to show the healing power of God. When God healed the blind man so he could see, God also brought spiritual sight to that community. When God healed Maleah, He brought a renewed faith to her family and all those who hear her testimony. Trials are often not about us; trials are about God.

Double Deliverance

GINA FLORES-CLARIDY

Then they cried unto the LORD in their trouble,
and he delivered them out of their distresses.

~Psalm 107:6 (KJV)

My mother died when I was about 12. My two younger sisters and I were placed with my aunt and uncle until my father won custody. That is another story. This one is about drugs and God's deliverance.

I remember being around 14 or 15 years old, taking the Greyhound bus to Miami to purchase what was then called "lids," an ounce of weed. I purchased four of them, which totaled a quarter pound. That was the beginning of my entrepreneurship in the drug business. Up until that point, I had smoked weed but had never sold it. From that point forward, it seemed like I sold one form or another of an illegal substance. It could have been weed, pills, powder cocaine, or rock cocaine (crack). I sold them and ran drugs from state to state.

Not only did I sell drugs, but I also used drugs—except pills. I thought I was a smart business and money manager. I always kept a steady job as well. Using crack cocaine was the worst thing I could have ever done. Using and selling crack cocaine led to me becoming a three-time felon. The first offense was a year's probation, which I violated. The second offense was a year in prison and two and a half years of probation. Eventually, I violated that too. I was on the run from the law with my younger boys, who were then about six and eight years old. I also had an older son, who was on his own.

After taking my younger boys to live with family members for a while, I was supposed to turn myself in to the authorities. I wanted to put the criminal behavior behind me, but I did not want to serve the year in jail, so instead of turning myself in, I ran—for seven years. Running from the law for so long was hard. I was always looking over my shoulder, always wondering if one of the people I knew would become angry with me and report me.

While traveling as a road manager for a gospel artist, I remember being at a venue where a man was watching me. As I walked closer to him, I realized I knew him. He could have taken me down right there, but he did not.

"I've been watching you and all the good you are doing," he said. "Be careful, watch your back and keep up the good work until the time comes to do what you must do." I was so thankful and grateful. I smiled in gratitude and left.

When my boys were about 15 and 17 years old, I believe that I heard God clearly: "This is your release, go!"

I made plans to return and deal with my law violations. My boys were old enough now. With the help of my oldest son, who was about 33 years old, we prepared.

The drugs were so difficult to kick. I tried repeatedly to stay out of jail and go with my family. I failed again and again. I know that God watched over me. I know people were praying for me. I was praying for myself, through all my sin and addiction. I just know God kept me. I knew that John 9:31 said something like God does not listen to sinners, but He listens to saints.* I recall plenty of times when I would finish my session getting high and my "get-high buddy" would drop me off, and I would read the Bible and pray for hours. I liked getting high, but I did not like myself high. I wanted to be free of this addiction so badly.

On another try for deliverance, I remember feeling like one of my sons was praying for me—I felt like I could feel him praying. This time, I went with my family from jail, and it was like instant deliverance. No drugs. No withdrawals. No dreams. No cravings. June 19, 2021 made twenty years clean. Not only was I delivered by God from drugs, but also from serving my time for the third offense. The prison sentence that I could have gotten was anywhere from 18 months to 35 years. For the probation violations and running from the law, I only spent 38 days in jail. The judge reduced the probation to one year, 120 hours of community service, fines, and restitution with terms of early release if I completed everything. In ten months, I completed everything and was released.

---

* John 9:31 (ESV) reads: *"We know that God does not listen to sinners, but if anyone is a worshiper of God and does his will, God listens to him."*

I always felt that there was favor all over my life. God poured out His love for me, even amidst my sin. He delivered me. For that, I am eternally grateful. The scripture that always gave me hope is Romans 5:3-5 (KJV), which states:

> *And not only so, but we glory in tribulations also: knowing that tribulation worketh patience; And patience, experience; and experience, hope: And hope maketh not ashamed; because the love of God is shed abroad in our hearts by the Holy Ghost which is given unto us.*

For Your Consideration

Sometimes, we get into habits, ways, and sins that take us away from God, but He loves us anyway. Others judge us because of prejudice and stereotypes, but Jesus accepts each of us just as we are. He showed love and compassion to the Samaritan woman who was living a sinful life, but Jesus loved her, nonetheless.

In John 4, the Bible discusses the interaction with Jesus and the woman at the well, a Samaritan, who was from a people with whom the Jews did not interact. Yet, Jesus—a Jew—was speaking with her. Not only was He speaking with her, but He also let her know that He knew all about her and her escapades with other Samaritan women's husbands, which made her community shun her. Nevertheless, Jesus received her and showed her loving kindness.

As the Samaritan woman and Jesus discussed worship, she told Him that she knows the Messiah is coming. Jesus replied: *"I that speak unto thee am he"* (John 4:26 KJV). She marveled that this was the Messiah. She hurriedly went back to town and summoned the Samaritans to see the man who told her everything about her life—this was her testimony. The Samaritans went to the well and saw Jesus. They asked Him to stay with them, and He did for two days, sharing with them about the Kingdom of God. Jesus used the Samaritan woman to share the gospel message to those in her village. She went from a sinner to a spiritual leader of her people. She recognized Jesus as divine. Jesus' love toward the Samaritan woman in all her sin demonstrates His love for all people.

As we struggle to unbind ourselves from sin, Jesus loves us. As we fail over and over, Jesus loves us. As we sit in the drug house, Jesus loves us. As we stand in the jail house, Jesus loves us. As we sleep in another's bed, Jesus loves us. As we lie, cheat or steal, Jesus loves us. Whatever our struggle, addiction, or shame, Jesus loves us. He is there for us and watching over us. Stay faithful to Him. Continue to worship Him. Dwell in His Word. Eventually, He will deliver us.

Awakened by a Miracle

STORMY WASHINGTON

And all things, whatsoever ye shall ask in prayer,
believing, ye shall receive.

~Matthew 21:22 (KJV)

I am reminded of the first time I witnessed a miracle firsthand. This was certainly not because God had not been amazing in my life. Quite the contrary. It is because He had been nothing short of amazing. That was when I began to truly understand the power of God and prayer.

I accepted Christ and began to consistently attend church when I was about 13 years old. Before then, I would attend because my parents required it. They loved the Lord and taught my siblings and me about Christ. They made sure we knew that Jesus died for our sins, loved us unconditionally, and would supply all our needs. They frequently reminded us that we should treat others the way we want to be treated. More than that, they taught us to extend the same grace to others that Christ extends to us. Although I believed everything I was told, this was different. I finally began to fully understand the purpose of having a relationship with the Lord. I became more serious about attending church. I was new in my walk with Christ and yearned to learn more about Him and His teachings. I would pray for direction and understanding of God's Word.

I knew the basic requirements of being a Christian, but to my knowledge had not experienced a miracle firsthand. As a young child, I thought waking every morning was automatic. As I matured in Christ, I understood that miracles occur every day. I came to believe that each day I wake up is not only a miracle but a blessing and a privilege.

When I was 14 years old, I often fell asleep listening to the radio or music on a cassette. I liked all types of music but rarely listened to gospel music. Like many young people, my favorite artists at the time were Luther Vandross and Natalie Cole. I loved the songs so much that they led me into disobedience that might have cost me my parents' respect and a friend.

I met my best friend when I was three years old, and she was two. When we were growing up, she would frequently let me borrow her boombox. That was a big deal back then. I had it by my side in bed listening to music. One night, my mother came into my room to say good night. She noticed the boombox in the bed and said, "Do not fall asleep with that radio in the bed."

"Yes ma'am," I replied. The next thing I remember was waking up to the sound of the machine hitting the floor. I immediately got up and turned on the light. I pushed play on the cassette player to see if it still worked. It did. I was relieved and immediately thanked God. Then, I noticed that one side of the handle had popped out. I felt a sick feeling in my stomach.

Now, my mother was by no means a mean woman, but she said what she meant and meant what she said. *How am I going to tell her what happened?* I thought. I did specifically what she told me not to do. As a result, she and my father would have to pay to replace the boombox.

My heart was pounding. I was nervous and disappointed. I felt that way because I deviated from my norm. I usually honored my mother by following her instruction. As a child, I was obedient to a fault. My parents would tell me what to do. That was all they had to do—tell me the rules or expectations. I would follow their words to a tee. I was anxious because I would have to tell my friend who trusted me with her boombox that I broke it. I tried feverishly to push the handle back into the groove to no avail. So, I began to do the only thing I knew to do—pray.

I do not remember my exact prayer, but I asked God for a miracle. Mark 9:23 (NIV) states: *"Everything is possible for one who believes."* I was familiar with some of the miracles in the Bible. The broken boombox handle seemed small compared to loaves of bread and fish that fed thousands or walking on water.

I already trusted and believed in God and the Word of God, so I truly believed He would answer my prayer. I asked God to fix the boombox. I asked for forgiveness for disobeying Mother. I truly believed that I knocked the machine off the bed and broke the handle because I disobeyed her. I was still nervous and disappointed, but I decided to act on my faith. I turned off the light, climbed back in the bed, and fell asleep with the boombox by my side. The last thing I remember before falling asleep was praying.

I woke up again to the sound of the boombox hitting the floor for a second time. I could not believe I did it again. I stood up and turned on the light. The machine looked as it did when it fell over the first time, only this time the handle was back in place. This was the first time that I experienced praying and seeing an immediate tangible response from God. I believed God could and would do it. My belief in God was strong. My desire to be a part of the church was strong, but I was stunned, nonetheless. Everything I was taught, read, and believed about God regarding faith and prayer manifested that night.

I heard a sermon on faith from James 2:26 (NKJV): *"Faith without works is dead."* The sermon is one of my favorites to this day. The preacher stressed the importance of believing that God can and will answer your prayers, no matter how great or small. I had no idea that all I heard and learned thus far would have such an amazing impact on my life. That experience was a pivotal point in my life during those teen years. It was amazing to me that even though I did not listen to spiritual or gospel music, or consider myself to be super-spiritual, God still honored my request.

I now know that God meets us where we are. He uses every situation to remind us of His power and grace. I believe that God knew I needed that experience as a teenager to help establish my spiritual foundation, deepen my faith, and strengthen my walk with Christ. I continue to marvel at the power of God and prayer.

For Your Consideration

Even when we think we are too insignificant for God to care about us and the little things that bother us, He does. He cares about us and everything that matters to us—the big things and the small things.

In the Book of Samuel, Hannah was a wife but not a mother. Even though she had a husband who loved her, her greatest desire was to be a mother. She waited, cried, and fasted. As much as she desired to get pregnant, it did not happen. Finally, she took her request to the Lord. In absolute anguish, she went to the temple and cried profusely. In 1 Samuel 1:11 (KJV), Hannah vowed:

> *O Lord of hosts, if thou wilt indeed look on the affliction of thine handmaid, and remember me, and not forget thine handmaid, but wilt give unto thine handmaid a man child, then I will give him unto the Lord all the days of his life, and there shall no razor come upon his head.*

After making her promise to God, she continued to pray silently with her lips moving, so it looked like she was drunk. She told Eli, the priest there, that she was not drunk but desperate, depressed, and distressed. Eli prayed that the Lord would grant Hannah's request and told her to go in peace.

Hannah believed in Eli's prayer, but more importantly, she believed God. She left in peace and arrived home to be with her husband. Soon thereafter, she was pregnant! The Lord answered her request. She delivered a son, Samuel, which means "asked of God." After Hannah weaned Samuel, she kept her promise to God. She brought her son back to the temple where she prayed for him, dedicated him to the Lord, and left him there to serve God. When Hannah prayed, made a vow to God, and changed her disposition, God answered.

From answering a prayer about having a child to fixing our radio, God is faithful. He cares about each big and little thing occurring in our lives. Psalm 56:8 (NLT) states: *"You keep track of all my sorrows. You have collected all my tears in your bottle. You have recorded each one in your book."* Nothing about our lives is too insignificant for God. He is not just concerned about our souls, but with our needs as well—down to the smallest things that preoccupy us and cause us distress. His love for us is so great that everything about us concerns Him. We can bring the most trivial concern to Him in prayer. He will hear and answer.

Living Single:
A Blessing in Patience

ANONYMOUS

But if we hope for what we do no yet have,
we wait for it patiently.

~Romans 8:25 (NIV)

I did not intend to spend my life living single. I admired my parents' marriage until they passed. I assumed that marriage would happen for me as well. Plus, it was a desire of my heart, and the Bible promises that if I delight myself in the Lord, then He shall give me the desires of my heart (Psalm 37:4 KJV). I understood that to be a conditional promise, but I had always delighted myself in the Lord, even when my actions were sometimes off track.

The *one* thing I always dreamed about was being a bride. As a young teen, I would draw my wedding and dream about my dress. I included the number of bridesmaids I would have. I wanted my colors to be peach and gold. I wanted nothing more than that. I am now over half a century old, and my dream wedding has still not manifested. I do not even care about colors at this point. I just want to be married. I am tired of marking "S" for "single" on every government or medical form that I have to complete. I am also tired of listing my cousin as my emergency contact because I have no husband.

My social media status reads "single." Year after year, there has been no change. I want to be able to update my status with "married," or at the very least "in a relationship." I would even settle for "It's complicated." But still no change. My social media memories are filled with exciting trips and vacations with sister friends. But I want a man—my own man—sent from God. I want someone to be there for me daily. I want a husband.

I am tired of praying. I am worn out from trying to live the perfect life for God to bless me with a good man. I am just tired. I feel so alone in my house and the world. I eat hot dogs and salads because I only cook for myself. I want to plan my meals and cook my man's favorite foods. I want to plan vacations and not be alone on holidays, but I have no one. The Christian walk is challenging. I volunteer. I tithe. I fellowship weekly at church. I read my Bible daily and meditate on the Word. Yet my one prayer, my one dream, still has not manifested.

I also really wanted children; I wanted them so badly that I considered an artificial fertilization procedure where I would not need a man. I decided against that, and eventually, my ability to birth my own child passed because life kept going. But God can still bring me a husband.

I feel like my heart is full of love to give to a nice man, but I do not have one. Each year, I pray and hope this will be the year. I see friends and foes marry, and I always claim, "I got next!" I believe it, but each year makes it more difficult to believe. My faith has waned. I wonder if God forgot about me. I still do not know why God would not do what was so easy for Him to do—bring me a wonderful husband. Forget wonderful, God has not even brought me a husband. I am tired of speaking in tongues. I feel broken and distressed. I want a Word from God. I want God to explain why I feel like He failed me. I know that God answered David. God answered Hannah. God answered Rebekah—why not me? Am I not as important as His people I read about in the Bible? I feel forsaken by God. I am mad at God.

Christians seem to always have an excuse and end with, "Hold on . . . God is going to do it." I am tired of waiting and afraid to share my feelings. The answers are too exhausting. I have heard: "Get busy in God," or "When God moves one thing, He will bring something even better." I have also heard: "The husband comes when you are in your purpose," or "God is preparing your husband," or "You need to be healed first." I am tired of the excuses. I just want to be married to a good man.

Is it that God has nobody who wanted to choose me as a wife? I ask myself, of all the people He created, He did not create any man for me? Out of nearly eight billion people in the world and over 300 million in the United States, half of them are men. God has not one man—just one—for me?

I am tired of trusting the process. I have trusted it, and to date, it has failed. I heard so many times, "There is someone out there who will love you." But, how come everyone around me seemed like God blessed them with a husband? What about me? I wanted to do God's will, and I felt I had been doing that. I have been active in church. I thought I was living my purpose. I have had times when I have been awfully disobedient, but for the most part, I live right. I have been busy, but still, I am single. I am so single that I tell people I am "single, single." They laugh when I say that, but I am serious.

Daily I say to myself: *Today could be the day when God turns it all around and brings my prince.* Day after day turns into year after year. Time waits for no one. I look at my face in the mirror and recall when I really started praying about this. Now, some 25 years later, my skin shows signs of my age, and the edges of my hair are graying. I still cling to hope, prayerful for a breakthrough. It is my turn! I wake in the wee hours of the morning and spread my hands on the other side of my bed that is filled with eyeglasses, books, and my computer. I want to feel the warm body of my husband. I reach out and pray on that side of the bed. At one time, I worshipped that side of the bed, but it stayed empty and ready for my man to arrive but that did not happen; now, it is filled with things. I refuse to even buy a king-size bed because it would be a constant reminder of the emptiness on "his" side.

I have other things to pray about, but nothing has been more pressing to me than praying for the manifestation of my husband. I wonder where he is, what he is doing now, how come he has not found me, what his name may be—my mind never stops wondering about every minute detail of this man I have in my head. I consider myself a mature Christian, but not in this part of my life. Here, I feel weak and immature. I am embarrassed at my level of faith. It has almost become nonexistent in this area of my life. Then I wonder, maybe that is the problem, but time has worn me out. Time has worn my faith out. I have been a bridesmaid more times than I can count. I want to be a bride. My mother wanted me to be a bride. My grandmother wanted me to be a bride. My father wanted me to be a bride. My brother still wants me to be a bride. Some accused me of being judgmental toward men, running them away. Someone always had an excuse—either spiritual or natural.

Sometimes, I go to public places, usually a restaurant, and observe couples or families, then imagine myself as the wife. I am embarrassed by this, but I want a man to want me so badly that nothing else matters. I have no tears left to cry about a husband. I am all dried out. I wish I could cry about it or release it some way, but I am dry. I pray for everyone else, but my own prayers have gone unanswered. No one knows really how disappointed and rejected I feel.

On a really challenging day, I called my good friend Nicole. She was one of my dearest friends and a confidante. I told her how I was upset with God. I shared how I felt that He disappointed me. She knew all my "husband" prayers and had fasted and prayed with me. She prayed for me on the spot:

God cover this woman of God. Strengthen her this day. Fill her up with Your love, joy, and peace. Let her know You are with her. Be her comfort when the days get hard, like today. Keep her on Your path. Allow her faith to be restored in You today. Sometimes it is hard but let her know You got her!! In Jesus' name, I pray, Amen.

After the prayer, I immediately felt better. I immediately felt renewed. I was determined to stay the course. I would not give up on God. Nicole reminded me of all that He had done for me and her. Plus, I really do believe that God will answer my prayer—this desire of my heart that never went away. It was a bit hard for Nicole to understand. She had been married for 20 years in an awful marriage—nothing like she ever imagined. She was eager to get a divorce as soon as her son went off to college. She estimated that she would lose half of her retirement in the divorce, but she wanted out so badly that she did not care. So, she was often quiet when I shared with her my desire for marriage. When I would tell her how I often felt lonely and alone, she nodded her head in agreement because she said she had felt that same way for most of her marriage.

"I don't think it's the singleness that's hard for you," Nicole said, "it's the loneliness you feel that you associate with singleness. Marriage, though, is not necessarily the cure. It could be. Marriage may work out for you, but it didn't for me. I have always felt lonely in it, and for the most part, I usually go places alone."

"You never shared this with me," I said.

"It's too embarrassing. Maybe I married the wrong man. I asked God for an honest man, and that is what I got but nothing more. I should have made a longer list because although my husband is honest, he has not been a good provider or emotionally available."

"Would counseling help?" I asked.

"I have my own issues, too. I learned in counseling that I was not patient with my husband, allowing him to be human and to have faults like the Bible says in Ephesians 4:2. I am laughing now because I will admit that I am much more spiritual and know God much more because of my marriage— maybe that was my lesson."

"Thanks for sharing."

"I hope God answers your prayer for marriage, but not just a marriage—a good marriage. So, I guess you don't remember when I told you years ago that I had just gotten engaged?" Nicole inquired.

"Not really, I remember the moment, but not what I said," I replied.

"You asked me 'What did God say?' I was puzzled because I never thought to ask Him whether my husband was the one He had for me. You and I were in our twenties, and I never even knew He would answer if I did, but I never did. That question—your question—has haunted me all my marriage."

"I am sorry that haunted you. I don't remember my words, only that I was always razor-sharp focused on trying to listen and follow God. But look where that has gotten me . . . a life of singleness," I replied.

"No, no . . . I am glad you asked," Nicole said. "I just wish I knew then how to ask and listen for an answer. I mean you are not married yet, but you also have not been in an awful marriage. Singleness may be hard, but it is not ugly like a bad marriage. Now I know why Paul said in First Corinthians 7 that singleness is a gift."

"How are *you* doing? I mean are *you* ok?" I inquired.

"Honestly, I think I am overweight and not in the best health because of my marriage. If you only knew half of what I have gone through with my husband. I wish I had followed up with questions to you about seeking God. I have been tormented by the notion that my husband was my idea and seemingly not God's, and that God would have made a better choice for me had I been open to listening or aware that God speaks to us or even cares so much that He would direct me in that."

"Yes, He cares a lot," I said. "I remember four times going to God about marriage because I was considering whether a current suitor was my husband. Each time, God said, 'No, that is not him,' and it was quickly evident that I heard God accurately. God protected me from four catastrophes for sure, and I am grateful to God for that. I guess it is always easier to think the grass is greener on the other side. But had you known singleness was a gift for you to be able to grow more in God, would you have put away your desire for it?"

"Honestly, I don't think so. No way," Nicole admitted. "I saw my parents married, and I wanted what they shared. And I wanted it badly. I almost saw singleness as some awful burden to bear. Like maybe people would think no one wants to be with me. Or maybe I am hard to love. I realize now that none of that is true. Looking back with my experience now, I say be patient. I know it's hard, but there is a blessing in patience—in waiting. I wish I had. Yes, I check the 'I've been married' box, but I'll also be checking the 'I've been divorced' box soon enough. People talk about singleness like it is the worst thing in the world, but I would give anything to wait on God. Wait, sis, God will do it for you. I bet He will even surprise you!"

"One of my friends once told me that she would prefer to be a divorcee rather than a spinster. I was disturbed by that," I said.

Nicole and I both laughed and said our goodbyes. I was encouraged after our call. I decided to go for a walk. I ended up at the local park to spend some time in nature, reminding myself of the awesomeness of God and all that He created. I knew that even though He had not yet answered my prayer, my faith believed it was on the way. I would trust the process. I would wait. I would not jump into any relationship that I knew did not resonate with my spirit. I would delight myself in the Lord and wait on God to fulfill the desire of my heart, and not just for a marriage, but for a *good* marriage. Until then, I would seek to flourish in my singleness and cherish each moment. I would not cry; I would wait, patiently and gracefully. And if God blesses me with a husband, then I will accept that, but he must be from God.

For Your Consideration

It is hard to wait. No one likes to wait, especially when we see others receive the very things we are desiring. But in the Bible, the psalmist beckons us to wait: *"Be still in the presence of the Lord, and wait patiently for him to act"* (Psalm 37:7 NLT). We are so anxious to jump ahead of God— to jump the broom or other desires— that we do not see why God was having us wait in the first place.

When we consider the people in the Bible, many waited for years and sometimes decades. Abraham waited for the promise of offspring with Sarah. Jacob waited seven years to be with Rachel. Joseph waited for his freedom. Mary waited to see Jesus as the Messiah. The Israelites waited to reach the Promised Land. Job waited in suffering to restore his family and property. David waited to be appointed as king. Even Jesus waited to begin His ministry. The Bible also includes examples of those who did not wait: Sarah encouraged Abraham to use her handmaiden, Hagar, to have a child because God was taking too long. It is hard to wait.

While we are waiting, we are to be still—to rest in the Lord. In the season of waiting, grow in God, meditate on His Word, spread His word, serve Him, cast our cares and anxieties upon Him, but do not step ahead of Him and try to manifest the

Word for ourselves. When we do this, we drift from God's will and plan for our lives. We may cause ourselves or others to suffer, and we may delay our blessings, and in the worst case, they are denied completely.

In the book of Samuel, Saul was impatient and disobedient in waiting on Samuel's arrival. As a result, Samuel chides Saul and tells him that he missed out on a magnificent reward: *"But now your kingdom must end, for the Lord has sought out a man after his own heart. The Lord has already appointed him to be the leader of his people, because you have not kept the Lord's command"* (1 Samuel 13:14 NLT).

When we jump ahead of God and carry out our own plans, we begin to question God and ourselves because we got what we wanted, but it is not bringing the joy we thought. We ask ourselves, *Did I step ahead of God? Was this what God wanted for me? Why do I have my desire, but remain miserable? What if I had waited? Who did God have for me as a spouse? I wonder what life would be like had I waited on God.*

In the book of John, Jesus said, *"You don't understand now what I am doing, but someday you will"* (John 13:7 NLT). Jesus' words are powerful instructions for us to wait because we do not know what He is doing, when He will do it, how He will do it, or why He will do it for us. We must trust God and be confident while we wait and believe God and His Word. Psalm 27:14 (NLT) reads: *"Wait patiently for the Lord. Be brave and courageous. Yes, wait patiently for the Lord."*

The Gift of Courage

SHARON Y. RILEY

Be strong and of a good courage, fear not, nor be afraid of them:
for the LORD thy God, he it is that doth go with thee;
he will not fail thee, nor forsake thee.

~Deuteronomy 31:6 (KJV)

I find that it is all right to feel what you feel, as long as your feelings do not force you to forfeit your future. Courage allows you to do that, to feel while forging ahead, and eventually, prepares you to become an encourager.

After sunset one February Friday evening, I placed a phone call. My response to the voice on the other end was, "Can you come pick up my mother?"

That day, I realized that courage is not taught. It is not something merely learned through precepts and principles. It is the conquering conscience awakened by an encounter. It is an experience endured. Courage was caught in my clutches as I tenaciously pursued an awareness of myself by desperately seeking God, the only One greater than anything or anyone I have ever known. Through confrontations, conquests, and challenges, I believed God's Word in Philippians 4:13 (NIV): *"I can do all this through him who gives me strength."*

*   *   *

The second hand's faint cadence on the wall clock invaded the waiting room's atmosphere as if it were a concrete hammer demolishing a neighborhood sidewalk. This was one of those days when even silence seemed loud. The warm air was sterile. The burnt orange couches, chairs, end tables, coffee table, television, telephone, and clock were strategically arranged into a typical living room setting. Countless families must have huddled in the private space for counseling, consulting, and consoling many times before us. Hospital waiting rooms host the wealthy, impoverished, broken, and brave similarly.

It does not matter how much you own or owe, how much you know or lack, every family that enters the space finds itself in need of a hope that lies between its heart and the pale blue hospital walls. Hope becomes your guide along the journey, the terrorist against the paralyzing thoughts in your mind. It is what makes your head turn whenever a white coat approaches the door. It is the lift underneath your armpit that helps you to the edge of your seat when the sound of footsteps in the tile-laden hallway draws close.

My immediate family and I arrived at the hospital like fresh spring rain. One drop at a time, we sprinkled throughout the waiting room. Each of us claimed a spot with an "I shall not be moved" disposition. That is a posture of determination that says no matter how long it takes, the answer will come, and I will be right here when it does. Everything is more intense and intentional with that mentality. We do not want to miss anything. We munch on a stockpile of snacks to avoid the need to leave for the cafeteria. We just want to be in place when the news arrives. We each want to hear the news for ourselves. Whatever it is. So, in that room the family waited, laughed, chatted, and napped, hoping for a favorable result on a biopsy.

This was not our first rodeo. Holidays, hospitals, and my mother were yoked like moisture on a raindrop. You just could not have one without the other. It was as if there were an astronomical alignment that coordinated the calendar and my mother's health. From Mother's Day to Thanksgiving or Christmas, we were either on our way to the hospital, on our way home from the hospital, or beside my mother's hospital bed, staring at a 13-inch television mounted where the pale blue wall and white ceiling met.

We started this day with a *why* in mind. *Why* did we choose to show up this day? We were commonly connected. *Why did we wait?* We were either afraid or courageous—uncertain of which. The unanswered question was the elephant in the room. So, we talked about many things, anything that came out of our mouths, except about *why*. We cracked jokes on one another, played the dozens, and made light of our dad's arm slipping off the right side of the chair, defeated by emotion and exhaustion. We just did not talk about our *why*.

Aunt Addie sat motionless, clenching her worn, double-strapped black purse across her stomach as if she were about to be robbed. Her legs were crossed at the ankle as she leaned to the left, resting her elbow on a waiting room chair that must have supported thousands of arms in its time. Periodically, she interjected pearls of wisdom into the banter between my siblings, Martha and Marcus, the family comedians. Her voice ascended over the chatter like an autumn fog above a pond in the wee hours of the morning.

"We're just going to believe God, that's all," Aunt Addie declared. "He's in control, and we've just got to trust Him."

Although highly revered, Aunt Addie was often secretly ridiculed. Whatever came out of her mouth sounded like a correction or scolding, in the name of Jesus. She was given the moniker "lord" because somewhere in her conversation, appeared a reference to Jesus or God. By the time she finished speaking, you felt like you were on your way to hell with gasoline drawers. Out of a fleeting conviction, the room grew quiet, but only long enough for the comedians to create another joke. Just as quickly as the morning sun evaporates the fog, her voice disappeared amidst everyone's laughter and chatter. That was coping. More than that, the chatter was hoping. We hoped that there was a remedy to whatever problem the doctors would find. At the same time, we wished they would find nothing at all.

The five o'clock evening news ushered a sense of sobriety into the room. The bright April sun peered through the blinds as if it waited with us for news from beyond those walls. Waiting morphed into worrying. Most of us grew tired of sitting but were too weary to stand. We began to shift in our seats and slouch down on a chair or couch until the nape of our necks rested on the back of the furniture. This is the in-between space where you are not really this or that. It is the creative space where you are trying to turn something into what it is not. You posture yourself to imagine what you want because what you have is no longer comfortable, convenient, or comforting. The imagination does not change what you have, it only temporarily makes you feel as if you have what you want. The one thing we all wanted by then was an answer. Our silenced chatter gave way to sighs, the limit of our capacity to wait.

Alongside the family, I felt the anxiety and anticipated the pain of disappointment. I held my breath. I am normally the absent one. That day I was present. The desire to know penetrated my will to wait. I gently slipped from my seat to enter the hallway, a never-ending corridor of white walls, closed doors, and mirrored floors. You know what it is like when someone estimates the time for something, and their time and your time are just not the same. My heart pounded against my chest, but I pretended against the fear to be ready to face the results of the biopsy.

Ten steps. I could finally breathe again, free from the pressure of managing the emotions of an entire room. My legs felt like logs. I shuffled across a threshold where the friction of Berber carpet flowed into the sleek tile as a babbling brook diminishes into a gently drifting stream. If I could just abandon anticipation and anxiety, we might all relax. Transition does not always give you time to relax. You just have to keep it moving. My neck tilted forward, drooping between my shoulders as my forehead lay parallel to the cold tile floor beneath my feet. I sighed and stared into my image that was glaring back at me from the floor. The image staring back at me from the floor bore the same pain, the same anxiety, and the same bewilderment that I saw in my sister, brothers, aunt, and our friends in the waiting room. Hope was fading and the oppressive thought of what could be dominated my mind.

The second hand on the clock faintly held its cadence in the distance while the clog-clad feet of a surgical nurse inadvertently synchronized with the tick-tock of time marching forward. An answer finally arrived. Something at this point was far better than the nothing we rehearsed the majority of the afternoon. The nurse, wearing a crisp, white, two-piece pants uniform presented herself through the doorway. She stopped just inside of the door frame, gliding one hand into the front pocket of her uniform.

"The doctor has finished the biopsy, and he is on his way to let you all know how things went," she said in a soft-spoken voice. "Your mom did well, and she is on her way to recovery. You will be able to go back and see her in about 45 minutes to an hour. In the meantime, can I get anything for anyone?" The only thing any of us wanted was an answer regarding my mother's condition. A staggering chorus of pleasant refusals echoed throughout the small waiting room, and the nurse turned and made her exit. The nurse was kind, pleasant, and obviously well-trained. She gave us no indication one way or another about what the doctor may say. She brought us neither hope nor disappointment, but she did deliver a lingering cloud of anticipation.

My hands became moist and clammy as an icy weighted blanket covered my insides, the signal of my evolving anticipation. Fear gripped my heart, but *"God has not given us a spirit of fear . . ."* (2 Timothy 1:7 NLT). I knew the assignment of sharing the news with our family was mine alone. I was the healthcare surrogate, the ICE (in case of emergency) contact. The temperature rose swiftly when the doors swung open. The head of the oncological surgery department stepped out. Six-foot-plus, the lean, brown-skinned doctor with almond-shaped eyes moved with confidence and grace beneath the turquoise scrubs and white coat. His face was blank. Unscripted. No smile. No frown. Every step that he took controlled the rhythm of time. The hallway seemed to grow longer. It was like watching a slow-motion movie. I wearily looked into his eyes and forced a smile. I struggled to raise my arm to shake the doctor's hand. It felt as if I donned five-pound weights on my wrists. This man held within his mouth and mind the only words that mattered to any of us at that moment. He walked with me toward the waiting room door. My older brother bravely stepped into the hallway, and we stood together, attentive, and anxious.

"The biopsy went well," he said. The surgeon's voice was authoritative and certain. "We were able to locate the tumor at the base of her brain. Because of where it's located, removing it will severely compromise her quality of life, and she most likely would be in a vegetative state for the rest of her life."

His words cut through my heart like a warm knife cutting through butter. Everything within me melted. A lump lodged in my throat. My lungs suspended the next breath. My tear ducts locked. I had neither breath nor tears. I was just numb; everything froze. My heart was screaming, *Nooooo!* My brother immediately left my side as a single tear streamed from the right corner of his right eye. He could not handle the thought of something being permanently wrong with our mother who rebounded on more occasions than we could remember. She was resilient. When she injured a toe, diabetes found a vulnerable place of expression. Eventually, she lost that toe, then half of that foot, and then the ankle. Circulation failed in the other leg almost five years later. Eventually, it was lost to another amputation. Now something in me was being amputated at that moment, my hope.

With every amputation, diagnosis, or dilemma, she bounced back. Her spirit was stronger than her circumstances. It did not matter what she had to lose. She fought to live. That is why the doctor's prediction was so perplexing. I quickly resolved within myself, *This isn't final.* My brother, who abandoned me in the hallway, silently retreated to the waiting room. His spirit was broken. He walked into startled faces, then stood in silence. As they noticed the declaration on my brother's face, tears puddled on his lower eyelids. He said, "It doesn't look good." No one spoke. There was not enough space in my emotions to manage anyone else's at that point. Whatever my family would feel, they would feel it temporarily without me. I was always available, but this time was different. I was officially, emotionally unavailable.

As I listened, I knew the only reason I could stand at all was that God stood up in me. It was my frame, my face, my heart, my emotions, and God's strength. The doctor asked if I had any questions. I guess I did. I did not know. I was stunned. My thoughts were bouncing around like a pinball looking for an exit. I was hurt. I was disappointed and heartbroken. I could not cry. I could not move. I could not do anything. My mouth began moving before my mind could catch up. I did have a question: "If you don't operate, how long will she live?"

"About nine months is the typical lifespan for this type of tumor." The doctor's lips moved, but I could only hear the voice of Charlie Brown's teacher: *It's a very aggressive form of cancer called wah-wa-wah-wa-wah-wa.* Whatever he said became a battle between vowels and consonants. Soundwaves dissipated into ambiguity. I could not tell if his voice was muffled, or if my ears were just rejecting any semblance of language. *How could something so horrible happen to someone so humble?* I asked myself. *She is loving and gentle, compassionate, and encouraging. This was a death sentence.*

He said she's going to die. She's not supposed to die. She recovers from everything. She's supposed to recover. I was angry, afraid, and anxious. How could I say to my family what was just conveyed to me? *Oh Lord, how am I going to do this?* "God, help me," I mumbled between clenched teeth. Only God could pull me through this. I could not think to ask the doctor to explain to my family what I had just heard. My heart was suspended between my ears, silently crying for someone to please help me. The doctor shook my hand firmly and said, "I'm sorry, there is nothing more that we can do. Good luck."

Luck??? Good Luck??? Is that what they say? Is that what they are trained to offer? Luck? I didn't need luck. I needed life. I needed my mother's life. I needed her to live. I needed her. So many thoughts went through my mind. The pressure rushed against my mind like a 300-pound linebacker. I stood in the pale sterility of the deserted hallway, not thinking or moving. I stood, as did my mother on her first prosthesis following the below-the-knee amputation of her right leg. Uncomfortable, yet she stood. How could I fall when she made standing seem so graceful? She did not wince or grimace. She was graced with this incredible gift to stand, even if she stood alone. Almost without thinking, my feet turned swiftly toward the waiting room door. I entered with news in my head that my heart was reluctant to share. My mouth opened, and the speech that I received from the doctor flowed across my lips into the atmosphere of anticipation. Verbatim, I repeated every word—nothing more, and nothing less. The room grew still.

My father, the man who swept my mother off her feet 33 years prior and married her in a backyard Jamaican ceremony near Montego Bay, sobbed inconsolably with his forehead cradled in his palms. Daddy was sometimes present, but many times absent as we grew up. He did not work out of town or travel for his career. He just was not present. He brought his paycheck home on Fridays, and we did not see him again until Sunday night or early Monday morning—when my mother would drive him to his job at the bakery. I always managed to wake up just in time to take the predawn ride across town in the back seat of the car. I do not remember why my mother drove my dad to work at such an ungodly hour. We always had two cars. To see his emotional response—while knowing this—was revealing. I was relieved to see him cry. Through all the ups and downs in their marriage, I was not sure if he had a heart for my mother at all.

My sister sat motionless. Her tear-kissed face drooped beneath the burden of my mother's fate. I could only imagine the depth of her dismay. Although she was an adult, my sister remained somewhat dependent on my mother for almost everything. Whenever she was in between places to live, my mother housed her and her children. If she needed groceries, a meal, money, a ride, encouragement, direction, or anything at all, my mother made it happen.

My brother walked silently out of the room. His career path followed my mother's. His food-dripped, black work boots fought with the cuffs of his black and white checkered restaurant pants as he exited the room. He learned to cook well at an early age. In elementary school, I always asked him to make my eggs because he scrambled them perfectly. They were always light and fluffy with plenty of flavor. He found his niche in the kitchen and made a living off what he gleaned from my mother's influence. He cut the apron strings by the time he graduated from high school and remained slightly distant, emotionally and physically, until now.

Everyone else in the room drew together with me and held one another in a clenching embrace, without words. Right ears rested on left shoulders. Left cheeks pressed into left cheeks. Sniffles interrupted the silence as we wrapped our arms around one another. Tears ran together. No adequate articulation of anyone's thoughts could compensate for the strength that we found in the deafening silence and strength of each other's presence. I collected my thoughts and said, "Let's pray, y'all." *After all, what else should we do?* I thought. We grabbed one another's hands and held on tightly, palm to palm. Forming a chain of hands and hearts, we gripped hands and vowed to be all right. With every head bowed, and every heart broken, we prayed through streaming tears. It was a given, I made the suggestion to pray, and in my family's eyes, I should be the one to lead the prayer. No one said this, but no one said anything else. After a deep sigh, I began to thank God for our mother. I confidently asked God for strength for our family and friends. There was a sincere, yet simple transmission of courage between us. We passed around the half-size boxes of durable, scratchy, hospital tissue. There were no more tears, and definitely no more tissues.

She was a wonderful mother. Mom infused strength and courage into our lives with her persevering spirit. She confronted challenges with an "I-can-do-this" kind of attitude. My mother seemed to find the positive in every negative. If anyone in her company needed anything at all, she always found a way to meet those needs. One of our first cousins took full advantage of the space of grace found in my mother's presence. When my cousin learned that she was pregnant with her first child, she drove 45 miles from her hometown just to sit at my mother's table to break the news. My mother created safe spaces for all of us to open our hearts. We could talk to her about almost anything, even when our revelations frustrated her, she managed to guide us without judging us.

My mother was an amazing wife. The love she gave never seemed to be reciprocated—not by any of us. She loved without limits. She complained about my dad throwing his money away, but our household never missed a beat because she was the difference-maker. By the time I was in middle school, I learned the reasons we stayed afloat. Mom remained responsible, making sure the bills were paid. Working both full-time and part-time jobs to make up the difference in the household income, she remained dutiful, making sure we were fed, dressed, and educated. She taught us to take care of ourselves, and a couple of us actually got it. She was influential. She housed several of our friends from time to time and convinced their mothers that they would be fine at our house. Her conversations with those mothers were disguised counseling sessions where she gave them tips on how to parent.

Everything that she represented, coupled with our faith in God, is the reason we were so hopeful. She always bounced back. She deserved to live, and God could make it happen. We believed. We trusted. She was not just our mother but our courage. That courage was on full display throughout her life as I knew it, especially during times of illness. I remember standing at the foot of her hospital bed after a week-long hospital stay. The doctor had just left the room, and I asked Mom if I could see her foot. I was always the fearless child. Nothing and no one intimidated me as I grew up (I learned that from my mother.). The top part of her foot was dark, black, blue, and purple. All her toes were caught up in what really looked like a piece of art. It did not look real at all. I put on a glove and touched it, thinking her toe may come off in my hand. It was the most disgusting thing I had ever seen, but my curiosity was intense. I gently moved it back and forth, and surprisingly, it remained intact. I placed the sheet in its original position, removed my gloves, and acted as if I had not seen a thing. When I asked her what the doctor's plan was, she replied, "I told him if it's dead, cut it off." She was bold, resolute, and resilient. I have taken those words and applied them to many situations in my own life, and in the lives of others: "If it's dead, cut it off."

My mother was our matriarch, our rock; we would always be fine as long as she was okay. She was our Big Mama from the movie *Soul Food*. The immediate decision before us was to determine who qualified to have an audience with our lady of grace on the heels of such a devastating revelation. No one volunteered, but I felt compelled. I was in elementary school when my mother was diagnosed with diabetes. It was natural for me to accompany her to doctors' visits when she allowed me to. I was smart. I listened well, and I learned quickly. In the third grade, I remember the nurse teaching me how to administer an insulin shot to my mother in the event she ever needed my help at home. If her blood glucose level dropped or became elevated, I was being equipped to assist. The nurse placed an orange in my hand, gave me a syringe filled with water in my other hand, and showed me how to penetrate the orange with a quick prick into the orange peel. Days later while at home, I asked if I could give my mother her shot. Surprisingly, she agreed. I embraced every issue of her health from that day forward. I thrust myself into her healthcare at an early age. I knew what medications she took and for what purposes. I knew the dosages. I knew her doctors' names. I knew what each specialist was responsible to handle. So, since I had always been in her healthcare corner, it was only natural that I would be her "corner man" this time. Every boxer or fighter in the ring has someone who cheers them on, helps to patch them up, and coaches them from outside of the corner of the ring. I cannot say that I ever coached her or patched her up, but I was indisputably in her corner cheering her to victory.

The evidence of our occupancy in the waiting room quickly disappeared. Everyone left to deal with their disappointment and to ponder the implications of the news that had just been revealed. What that really meant was somebody needed a couple of cigarettes; somebody needed a joint; somebody needed a drink; and somebody needed to just be left alone.

No one wanted to approach my mother with tears because they knew she needed strength that they could not immediately provide. Between fear and fatigue, they were all spent. Rising to meet the next challenge, I seized the privilege of sharing with our mother what she faithfully shared with each of us—the gift of courage. I believe her courage stemmed from her faith in God. She prayed a lot. She read the Bible often and was faithful in church attendance all my life. She confidently believed in God's ability to work out every issue. Whatever God did or allowed, and however He did it, was fine with her.

Like her, I prayed a lot. I talked to God under my breath as a child. He knew my secrets, my fears, and my frustrations. Whenever my father yelled because he could not find his keys, I prayed under my breath and my cover in bed, waiting for the yelling to stop and for the keys to be found. Miraculously, they were always found. I learned early that God listens and that His Word is true. He does what He says.

Mother's dimly lit hospital room was divided by a thin, bleached curtain suspended on a curvy rail. Her roommate sat quietly on the other side of the curtain with the television volume on low as to not disturb my mother's side of the room.

I walked in after taking a deep breath, and I stood at her bedside with my hand resting on the cold bed rail. Our eyes met. She opened her mouth. Out came the sound of syllables muffled with tears. Through the jumbled, broken speech, I heard her say, "I have cancer." She sobbed for almost a minute, and then she became silent. Her face was blank. I know she was as shocked as the rest of us. It was overwhelming because our mother did not cry often. It took a lot to draw out her vulnerability. I sat down in the chair beside her bed and placed my right hand on her left forearm as she gently shook from the force of her tears. I watched without saying a word. I did not know what to say. The word cancer was so final, so fatal. I felt as if I were riding a train at a theme park, and it had just hit a brick wall. I did not know what questions to ask. I did not really know what this meant for our family at this point. *Was she going to live? Was she going to die? What would the treatment be? Would it work?*

My mind was bombarded with questions that I could not answer. The surgeon said she would live about nine months. Was there any possibility that he could be wrong, that something could change for the better? She cast her eyes down as if to avoid looking into my eyes. "It's ok, Mama," I whispered. I sensed for the first time that she was really afraid. So was I. I passed her a tissue. We sat without speaking. Our mother dried the tears from her face and neck, wadded the tissue into a little ball, and I turned my palm up to receive it, only to hear her say, "Cook something for your daddy."

How in the world? I screamed inside. That is the cleanest way I can say it. How does she come through what she just experienced, and consider someone else's needs above her own? I was angry. I felt that he did not deserve any attention or care. Her instruction was almost dismissive. I knew she probably needed space to deal with her own emotions, but "cook something for your daddy?"

He could cook, but he rarely did. He did not have to cook. My mother made sure he never missed a meal, even if she cooked it and left it on the warmer until he returned home. This was an old-fashioned lesson that she learned from her mother. She passed it down to us. I think she was giving me short-term and long-term instructions, making me commit to doing what she taught. Besides, my dad would only eat my mother's cooking and mine. Most likely she was just being who she is. My mother was courageous and compassionate, even in the face of calamity. One of her mantras was: "It is what it is."

Considering her disposition, I felt the need to be who she was. She was my perfect and most present example of what I felt a woman was supposed to be. I only needed to model her behavior. She was strong: I could be that. She was bold: I could be that. She was fearless: I was already that. It all seemed to work for her, so I adopted it. In about nine months her life could possibly be over, and someone needed to do what she did. Her absence would create a void, an empty space. We could not have that. We had a family to raise, and I felt responsible for making sure that happened. It was my obligation to step into the role my mother was about to vacate. Cook for my father, pay his bills, manage his household, watch out for my nephew, help my siblings, and take care of myself. All I needed to do was exactly what she did, just keep it moving.

I did just that. I managed her life for the next nine months. I scheduled her doctors' appointments but never accompanied her to one of them. I paid her bills, bought her groceries, coordinated her care at home, bathed her, cooked for her, shopped for her, and protected her as much as I could. At the end of nine months, I realized that I was becoming just like her. I was learning to exhibit strength in the face of pain. I was developing indomitable courage. I only realized it when I went from funeral home to funeral home on a solo journey to make funeral arrangements before she passed. I became more courageous with the fulfillment of every task that she asked me to complete. At some point, courage trains you to become an encourager. I kept life moving. That is what courage does. It keeps you moving, even when you feel like stopping. It helps you to realize that where you are is only a moment in the larger scheme of life, and if you just keep moving, that moment will soon be behind you. Courage provokes you to hope and search for the next moment or the next opportunity to experience something better or to become greater.

Nine months gives you a long time to reflect as you are moving. Not only did I reflect, but I grieved. My grief did not paralyze me because I had to remain present and productive. I could not even think about quitting because it was just not an option for me. I had too many responsibilities, too many people relying on me, and I had to keep it moving, even while mourning. Periodically, I mourned in anticipation of the impending emptiness, but I kept it moving by maximizing moments. Every holiday in the nine-month period became a major celebration. Fridays and Sundays were crafted family gatherings with the presence of food, family, and friends.

*   *   *

On this particular Friday evening, family members were gathered at our family's home because we planned to share a meal and hang out. I grabbed a few bags of frozen wings and soft drinks from the grocery store and rushed to the house. There was nothing unusual because we planned to gather, so there should have been multiple cars and people sitting and standing around outside. It was a little after six o'clock in the evening; the sun had not set because time had not changed yet. I made my way into the house, and I noticed the somber look on the faces of everyone I passed. No one said anything; they just looked at me. I greeted my uncle, hugged my aunt, spoke to my cousins, and kept moving. With every step, I was getting closer to our mother's bedroom. My sister, a family friend, our father, and our five-year-old nephew were all seated in our mother's room. I walked over to her bedside and touched my mother's right forearm, patting it gently.

"Hey," I said.

Our five-year-old nephew slid off the foot of the bed and walked over to me. He looked up at me and said, "Auntie, she passed."

"But she's still warm," I replied. Our family friend, who was also a nursing assistant responded, "She just passed about 20 minutes ago. I've already called hospice."

The only thing I could say was, "Oh, okay." I was shocked by the news but prepared for the process. I did not cry; I just stood there for a few seconds calculating my next move.

My sister looked up with heaviness written across her face and said, "We tried to call you."

I was okay. I studied the hospice instructions daily. I knew the process, and I marked each change. I knew her transition was near, but today? I reached into my purse and pulled out my phone, "Can you come pick up my mother?" I asked.

*   *   *

The nine months were over. I knew this day was coming, and I dreaded every bit of it. But I was not the same person in the end. Watching my mother endure the nine months left me with something that I did not start with. It was almost as if the courage I saw in her transferred to me. The courage that I developed was a God-given gift that our mother demonstrated and deposited into our lives. Every calamity or catastrophe is mysteriously laced with a strength and confidence that gives us the courage to hope and live. While the tears are flowing, it is hard to recognize how courageous you may have become; however, when the tears stop and you begin to process your emotions, you will find that you are stronger and wiser. And somehow during this process of pain and purpose, you realize that you got the gift—the gift of courage—a gift to use to encourage someone else.

For Your Consideration

Sometimes we are given real-life encounters that display the sovereignty of God. He does not always answer our prayers in the way we want, expect, or feel that we need. When this happens, our emotions can cause us to become angry with God. In that emotional space, we feel justified by "having an attitude" with God. Sometimes, what God allows will disappoint us. We blame ourselves, then question Him. We do not understand the sickness when the person who needs a cure is such a wonderful person to us. We sometimes wonder why God did not take another person who has been a terror on earth. We do not understand why God could allow someone who was so dedicated and committed to her family and Him to not finish living out her life for as long as *we* think she should have lived. We wonder why God would even think about taking someone from us who *we* think we still need. Inside we are yelling, *We were not ready!* But He took our loved one away anyhow. We know that our anger with God is unproductive, but we sometimes feel that He is the one ultimately responsible for everything. After all, He is omnipotent and can do anything! He could have intervened and altered the course of events, but He did not.

Being angry with God is an easy way out. We want to place the blame for our pain on someone. We question why God healed somebody else's loved one but allowed ours to die. We wrestle with why our marriage failed, yet others we know are still thriving in their marriages. We challenge why God allowed a mother to birth five children when another hopeful mother is longing to conceive. *Why Lord?* And, when we really delve deep, we are not really angry with God but angry because we cannot control the situation. We cannot make the situation any better. We feel helpless. Situations make us rely on God.

In these times of trials, God is our source of strength. Even amidst despair, God is there for us. It is true that *"all things work together for good to them that love God, to them who are the called according to his purpose"* (Romans 8:28 KJV). We just do not see any good at the moment of our pain, but He is there and will bring us out.

This story reminds us of Job in the Bible. He had everything and lived righteously. The devil told God that Job only acted that way because God favored Job. The devil believed that if he could inflict Job with suffering, then Job would curse God. God allowed the devil to take everything away from Job to show the devil that Job would still hold on to what he knew about his loving God. The devil killed Job's ten children, servants, and sheep, and inflicted Job with terrible bodily sores. Job's wife told him to curse God and his friends surmised that Job must have sinned and done evil things, but Job knew he was blameless. Job became bitter, anguished, and scared. He did not understand why God would allow evil people to prosper and allow people who live for God to suffer. Job wanted an answer from God but could not physically find God. Eventually, God intervened and restored Job's family, health, and wealth to more than he had before. But Job never really understood God. Rather, Job accepted the limits of human understanding. Notwithstanding all his suffering, Job never left God or his belief in God. Job said: *"Naked came I out of my mother's womb, and naked shall I return thither: the LORD gave, and the LORD hath taken away; blessed be the name of the LORD"* (Job 1:21 KJV).

A Prayer-Answerin' God

PAT VALENTINE

Then shall ye call upon me, and ye shall go and pray unto me,
and I will hearken unto you.

~Jeremiah 29:12 (KJV)

I believe we go into surgery with the fear of the unknown. I just know I trust God. Have your intimate moment with the Lord before the operation, and let Him be your peace.

I joined the Agapé Perfecting Praise & Worship Center in June of 2003. Since becoming a member, I have undergone several major surgeries. Each time I follow what it states in Proverbs 3:5-6 (NIV): *"Trust in the Lord with all your heart and lean not on your own understanding; in all your ways submit to him, and he will make your paths straight."*

In 2007, I had surgery in Birmingham, Alabama, and was supposed to be released the same day. Well, that did not happen. At the time of my release, my doctor went into an emergency surgery with another patient. So, it passed the time of my release, which went into another day. Once it hit twenty-four hours, there is normally another day charge—an additional $15,000. The doctor came in and apologized for being late. He said he would cover the extra day's charges. I knew it was the Lord's doing because 1 Timothy 6:17 (NIV) instructs that we should not "put *[our] hope in wealth, which is so uncertain, but in God, who richly provides us with everything for our enjoyment.*"

After being discharged, I made sure to take the medicine for pain. I took one of them as soon as I reached home. I had a hard time breathing shortly thereafter, which was a little frightening for me. My friend called the doctor to inform him of this symptom. He responded that it was of a side effect of the medicine, and that he would call in a lower dose of the prescription. I informed my friend I would not need to take anything, and she informed the doctor, who advised me to let him know if the pain became intolerable. I told her I would just pray and believe God. We could handle the surgery together. After the one pill and the side effect, I did not take any other pills for pain. I never experienced any pain after that. To God be the glory!

In October of 2017, I had another surgery. I prayed and asked the Lord to give me a word of comfort from the Bible. I was having my devotion the day before the surgery. The passage was Deuteronomy 31:8 (NIV): "*The Lord himself goes before you and will be with you; he will never leave you nor forsake you. Do not be afraid; do not be discouraged.*" At that very moment, I knew everything was all right. I felt the Lord cover me with a blanket of peace. From the surgery I never had any pain, nor did I have to take any medicine. Even the doctor was amazed by the fact that I did not have to use anything for pain. I know without a doubt, He is a prayer-answerin' God.

For Your Consideration

Often, we recite the verse, *"With men this is impossible; but with God all things are possible"* (Matthew 19:26 KJV). But sometimes, we recite it without really believing that God can do all things. He can if we let Him.

There are many miracles in the Bible. They are examples of what God can do if we let Him. God shows us a part of who He is through these miracles. He does not need a human or nature to perform these miracles, although sometimes He works through both. God shows us in His many miracles that He is a healer. In Mark 5, we learn about a woman who was sick with an issue of blood for 12 years. She saw many doctors for her bleeding condition and spent all she had, but her condition worsened. Then, she tried Jesus. She believed that if she just touched the hem of His garment, she would be healed. And she was! She had huge faith merely that touching the bottom of Jesus' garment would make her whole. Jesus said, *"Daughter thy faith hath made thee whole; go in peace, and be whole of thy plague"* (Mark 5:34 KJV).

One of the most common prayers is that of people praying for a cure for their own sicknesses or a loved one's disease. So many people need healing. People can have all the prosperity in the world, but without good health, it is hard to enjoy life. Jesus promises healing for our bodies and our broken hearts. We must believe Him, just as the woman with the issue of blood did after she had done everything else in her control to be healed. Perhaps she would not have had the ability to believe if she still had her money and doctors to rely upon, but all of that was gone when she heard about Jesus. Jesus healed her because of her faith.

Every person innately carries the measure of faith issued by God. We witness the measure of faith in the incessant cry of an uncomfortable baby. The expectant child wails until the diaper is changed or the bottle is warmed. With each need, the child repeats the behavior with the same expectation that someone will offer the necessary attention to satisfy his or her need. Each question or dilemma represented in our lives has a corresponding answer or resolution. God is able to do more than we can ask, think, or imagine. He is patiently waiting for us to acknowledge His ability, ask Him in faith, and accept His appropriate response to our dilemma. When we do, He outsizes our faith with His wonderful surprises. Remember the book of Matthew 21:22 (ESV) states, *"And whatever you ask in prayer, you will receive, if you have faith."*

Liberation from Loneliness

ANONYMOUS

And ye shall seek me, and find me,
when ye shall search for me with all your heart.

~Jeremiah 29:13 (KJV)

I did everything not to feel the pain of loneliness. I worked long hours for the corporation. I planned more social outings with friends. I shopped online in the wee hours of the morning. I talked on the phone more than usual. I did everything to fill the empty space of my days. I could not bear to feel the pangs of loneliness day after day. I had this unquenchable desire for connectivity, but few experiences of it. I felt lonely, empty, meaningless, purposeless. . . . What did God have for me? How can I be so "busy," yet be so empty? Most days, I felt drained, distracted, and angry. I kept hearing how solitude should feel creative, peaceful, and rejuvenating, but I jumped through hoops daily to stay busy, to fill my days, so that I would not feel the deep feelings of loneliness.

I felt this way before. This loneliness drove me to marry my husband. He is a good man and met all the checkmarks I had for a husband. Although this new union filled the intimate attachment of a romantic partner, the marriage did not mask the loneliness I felt. That was disappointing. "You have never felt lonely until you have felt that way in a marriage," a married friend, Brenda, told me before I merged my life with this husband-to-be. But I could not understand her comment because I just knew that my loneliness would be cured with the fulfillment of my desire for marriage. Married women often discourage single women from matrimony. I married, and for a short while, I felt satisfied, but it was not long before I realized that the marriage did not address my feelings of loneliness. Maybe if I had a child, I would feel fulfilled. So, after some fruitless attempts, I became pregnant and had twins. I loved the social gatherings surrounding the babies—the baby showers, the gender reveal parties. I loved the attention from all of this, and I believed I felt satisfied for a while. However, it was not long after that I realized not even the twins could cover up the feelings of loneliness I had. Honestly, I was jealous of the alone time that I saw my single, childless friends enjoy. I still longed for a deeper connectivity that I was not experiencing through marriage or motherhood.

I dove into work and spent numerous hours on the job. I thought maybe my loneliness was because my career no longer aligned with marriage and motherhood. My work paid off, and I obtained the desired promotion that I longed to have. I had new colleagues to get to know, both at the job and at happy hours following work. In the beginning, these interactions were new and exciting and seemed fulfilling. In reality, those were co-workers with different interests and obligations. I knew co-workers should stay co-workers and not cross into the friend zone, so I cut back on the gatherings.

I suggested to my husband that we buy the twins a dog because I thought they would enjoy one. The truth is I wanted an animal. I knew animals made great companions, and because nothing else was working, I wanted to try an animal. We purchased a puppy, and the twins enjoyed it, as did I. Yet, I still felt a deep loneliness that was unbearable. I went back to school to obtain a graduate degree in my field. I enjoyed the school group projects and the new challenges. I pressured myself to study harder than everyone else to get the best grades. The professor often mentioned my name because of my work product. I excelled in school, and my family was really proud of me. I liked planning my graduation party and the attention it brought. For a time, this kept me from thinking about the loneliness I often felt.

My life was full. I was very busy. I had a husband, twins, a dog, an admirable career, and another degree. Others would observe these events and accomplishments and often comment about how perfect my life was. From the outside, it appeared that way. I appeared busy and blessed, and I was, but I still could not shake the loneliness. I always had a prayer closet but did not use it often. When I did, I would sit in it and tell God about what I wanted to have or accomplish next. I wanted more each time I entered my prayer closet. The things for which I prayed, I watched as God manifested them, but the things did not mask my emptiness in the long term. Companionship and personal accomplishments filled some voids but not the deep loneliness I felt daily. So, I would add to the list—a newer car, a bigger house, more jewelry . . . Material things—stuff—only masked my profound sense of loneliness, but it never healed it. I felt trapped. I felt depressed and despondent. I felt that my feelings of loneliness swallowed my joy and darkened my life. I saw no way out of this life that everyone else saw as blessed. I felt embarrassed and ungrateful. I knew a shift was needed.

I began waking up early and going to my prayer closet. I no longer gave God a list of wants and desires; instead, I started out just sitting quietly, being grateful and listening. I had lots to be grateful for—a good husband, healthy twins, a prosperous career, my own good health, and that of my husband and our extended family. I began thanking God for what I had and for what He had done in my life. I also decided to relinquish the role of "superwoman" on the job. I was still committed to a spirit of excellence, but I would delegate more and come home earlier to show gratitude for what God had given me. I knew so many women who wanted to be married and enjoy motherhood as well, but they had not yet had those experiences. I knew they associated their loneliness with lack of marriage, motherhood, or money, but I wanted to tell them that those things cannot fill a void that God is meant to fill. I knew firsthand.

I began searching the scriptures and meditating on them. The scriptures that really piqued my interest were the ones about seeking God's face. I found nearly 100 scriptures and tagged each one in the Bible. Meditating on those scriptures, I realized I had mishandled my relationship with God. I also saw various scriptures that spoke about empty vessels. I understood that God wanted to fill the voids in my life. He works miracles in emptiness. Only He can erase the debilitating feelings of emptiness. When I was wondering how to move forward from what I was feeling and experiencing in my life, it was only God who could move me forward. I had to stop focusing on the emptiness and start focusing on the miraculous. I realized that I had been busy but not purposeful and that God was waiting for me to reach empty so that He could use me for His purpose.

I expressed to God what He already knew—I was emotionally bankrupt, empty, and lonely. So, I invited God into my life and asked Him to save me. I poured out my heart to God. I released my brokenness, my broken heart, my exhaustion, my disappointment. . . . Whatever I felt, I poured out to God. Nothing I had tried worked, so I poured out to God. I began to expect Him to move in my life, to redirect my path, and to *"make the crooked places straight"* (Isaiah 45:2 KJV). I began to really seek God's face, desire His presence, and want His purposes fulfilled in my life.

Busyness prevented me from reflecting on my life. Busyness intervened between God and me. Busyness disrupted my worship and communion with God. Busyness made me feel that I was productive, peaceful, and prosperous, but I was always striving for some other kind of satisfaction. Busyness confined me, blocked my transition into being greater in God, constrained me, limited me, and confused my purpose in God. I made a shift. I prioritized my worship, prayer, and communion with God. I no longer went to my prayer closet with a list of things. Now, I went to meet Him there—to seek His face. I realized that the connection I was seeking was a deeper connection with God. With this connection, whether I experienced marriage, motherhood, prosperity, or success, I would be just fine.

For Your Consideration

Feeling empty or lonely is more common than most people might think. At times, we have even considered suicide to quell the pain of loneliness. Maybe things about which we have prayed were received, but those answered prayers did not bring the fulfillment we thought they should. Perhaps we are still praying about things we think we need or want, and those have not manifested, so we blame our unfulfillment on unanswered prayers.

In the book of Kings, the Prophet Elijah begged the Lord to take his life in a suicide prayer. The verse reads: *"But he himself went a day's journey into the wilderness, and came and sat down under a juniper tree: and he requested for himself that he might die; and said, It is enough; now, O LORD, take away my life; for I am not better than my fathers"* (1 Kings 19:4 KJV). This is a remarkable request for a man who was so instrumental in partnering with God to manifest the miraculous. By being obedient to God, Elijah was fed by the ravens, controlled the weather, provided meals endlessly for the widow at Zarephath, revived her dead son, and defeated the prophets of Baal. Surely, Elijah was a witness and a participant to the power of prayer and provision of God. Yet soon after defeating the prophets of Baal, Elijah was threatened by Jezebel, and left to be by himself. He begged for God to take his life (1 Kings 19:1-3 KJV). This does not make sense for a man who was a witness to the many miracles of God. How could Elijah be so desperate and despondent now? Of all people, Elijah knew the power of God.

Instead of granting Elijah's death wish, God sent His angels to nourish Elijah for an upcoming 40-day sojourn to the mountain of God. When Elijah arrived at Mt. Horeb, the mountain of God, the Lord asked Elijah what he was doing there? Rather than reminding God of the obvious, Elijah responded twice: *"I have zealously served the LORD God Almighty. But the people of Israel have broken their covenant with you, torn down your altars, and killed every one of your prophets. I am the only one left, and now they are trying to kill me, too"* (1 Kings 19:10, 14 NLT). Elijah was lamenting that he did all God asked him to do, but it did not change the hearts of the Israelites. Now, Elijah himself was being hunted; he had had enough.

Have you ever been obedient to God, even when you did not understand, because you were expecting a certain outcome? Have you ever prayed for something and attained it, but you thought that you would feel differently when you received it? Maybe it was a marriage, motherhood, ministry, whatever. You are being a good wife; you are being a good mother; and you are serving God. Yet, there are still pangs of emptiness. Elijah became so depressed after having done so much for God, zealously following God's instructions, that he was now wondering what difference all his efforts had made. To him, it seemed like none. These are the times when we need to ask ourselves what God asked Elijah: *"What are you doing here, Elijah?"* (1 Kings 19: 9, 13 NLT). Ask yourself: *Where are you? What have you been doing? Who have you been spending time with? Where have you been spending your time? How have you been spending your time? Have you excluded God from your life? Are you reading and meditating on the Word of God? Or are you still handing God a litany of petitions to fulfill?* When we ask ourselves these questions, the honest answers may not always come from within our own minds. We may need to pray to God and allow the Holy Spirit to reveal to us where we really are and why we are there.

God revealed Himself to Elijah in a still small voice, letting Elijah know that God had been there all the time. Elijah was consumed emotionally with his own cares and fears, and completely forgot about the prophets who were being protected by Obadiah and the people who worshipped the Lord on Mt. Carmel. Elijah was not alone, ever. Elijah was not the only one left. God gave Elijah new instructions and told him that He *"will preserve 7,000 others in Israel who have never bowed down to Baal or kissed him"* (1 Kings 19:18 NLT). Elijah's new instructions required a renewed commitment. In other words, keep moving, keep following God, do not give up because it has not yet turned out the way you expected, hold on. Elijah felt lonely as if he were the only one feeling and thinking the way he was. Elijah had no idea what God was doing.

Pay attention to God's still small voice. Let Him lead and guide us through our feelings of emptiness and loneliness. The inner conflict that we sometimes face is a tool that God can use to sharpen our character and condition us for the greater things that He has called us to accomplish. We can feel lonely even when we are not alone. We can obey God, even when we do not understand. He can revive and rejuvenate us. He can rehydrate our thirst for Him. Only He can liberate us from the loneliness that is invisible to the world but haunts us internally. Only God.

Triumphant Not Tarnished

ISHNÉ K. HOBBS

In this you greatly rejoice, though now for a little while,
if need be, you have been grieved by various trials.

~1 Peter 1:6 (NKJV)

I spent the last few months making a list of everything I intended to do as soon as I turned 40 years old. This list would become my "40 while 40" agenda where I planned several activities for my upcoming year-long 40th birthday celebration. It was a list of everything I had not done that I needed to do and everything I wanted to do. I was excited. I was ready. This would be my time, my year. So, when my doctor gave me some life-changing news, I spent the following few weeks trying to unhear what I could not believe I heard.

"You have breast cancer," my doctor said.

I think I had an out-of-body experience. My heart stopped. Everything after that sounded like a loud echo coming from a tunnel: "Chemotherapy. Radiation. Surgery. Mastectomy. Appointments. Oncologist. MRI. Ultrasound. Mammogram." The words seemed jumbled together into one big blur. *Did she just say what I thought she said? No, I do not. Who me? I do not have cancer. I do not have time for cancer. What does that mean? What about my life? Who would help me even if I did have cancer? So, I cannot possibly have cancer.* These were some of my thoughts, as I tried to collect myself.

Getting a mammogram was on my "40 while 40" agenda along with other annual exams that I missed or had yet to schedule. I felt healthy, so I did not make my health a priority. I knew cancer ran in my family, and it was recommended that I receive a mammogram about four years prior, but I was feeling fine. Although I ignored the recommendation, I made sure it was at the top of my "40 while 40" agenda. A day after I turned forty, I went to my primary care doctor, who I had not seen for the past two years. We discussed a few things, including a lump I felt, and then she performed a routine physical exam. Looking back, I thought I felt a lump in my breast several months before I turned 40. However, I had just finished dealing with some "female" issues, so the lump was overlooked. After some further conversation with my doctor, she felt the same lump I noticed and immediately sent me for a mammogram. A few days later, I was called back in for a biopsy. Nearly a week later, my primary care doctor called me in the morning with instructions to come see her that same afternoon, and not to come alone.

"I got the results back from your exam," my doctor said as she moved from behind her desk to sit next to me. "I want to let you know that you have breast cancer. We caught it early but need to move fast."

My best friend was with me at the appointment. I should have known something was gravely wrong when my doctor told me not to come alone, but I just could not imagine cancer. My best friend heard the diagnosis as I was still trying to unhear or understand what I heard. I was just confused. I went numb. I drew a blank. With a look of shock and puzzlement, my best friend and I just became a ball of tears. We cried together. She held me while I cried, still trying to process what we had heard. I did not even try to comprehend the trial that was ahead of me. I was speechless. I could not utter a word, even if I tried. My primary care doctor told me that she was referring me to the best surgeon she knew. *Surgeon*, I thought. *Why do I need a surgeon?*

Trials were not new for me. I had overcome various hardships in my life, and I was proud of myself for completing college and being a single mom, among other things. But now I thought this was my time. Most of the other things I went through in my life, I had some control over them, I thought. But cancer sounded like an end—like something way beyond my control. From what I knew, many who had cancer desperately fought to live. Some made it through the fight, and some did not. *Would I be one of those? Would I die, too,* I wondered. *Cancer was out of my league. I could not do this alone. If God did not help me, then I would not make it.*

A few days after this devastating meeting with my primary care doctor, I met the surgeon. He spoke about cancer in a way that seemed like a foreign language to me. He used many acronyms. I felt as though I was back in this tunnel again like when my primary care doctor told me I had cancer. The words the surgeon used were abbreviations for words I did not know:

MM, MX, OS, and others. I mentally "checked out." Upon leaving his office, he said he would have an oncologist contact me to schedule an appointment. I walked away more confused and unsure of the next steps.

Within days, a scheduler called to ask me about what oncologist I wanted to use, as though I even knew one. The process was daunting. I was overwhelmed. I could not grasp what was happening or soon to happen. Things were moving fast, and I felt helpless. Then, the breast care coordinator called to answer my questions. She said it appeared as if I was confused about the process.

"Yes," I said. "I don't know what is going on. I keep hearing the word 'surgery,' but no one is explaining to me what is happening. I am still not comprehending this care plan. I don't know an oncologist. I haven't had a chance to review any. Why would I have?"

The care coordinator provided some names of oncologists, and I chose the only female name that she gave me. I did not know the oncologist, nor did I have a chance to review her. I just knew she was a woman. The coordinator spoke highly of the woman oncologist, so I felt that I might like her.

I was scheduled to see the oncologist shortly thereafter. I knew I had cancer but not its stage. The oncologist was the one who told me that I had stage 2 breast cancer and determined the treatment plan that I would have. Things that seemed confusing to me were becoming clearer finally.

"Chemotherapy. Surgery. Radiation," the oncologist told me. "That will be your plan."

Even though I could understand more, I was still in a daze. It had been weeks now, but I was still trying to process that cancer was part of my being. Everything was unknown. I had no clue how the process worked. I had so many doctor visits and tests to complete. I had never experienced surgery before. I had no idea how to do chemotherapy. I wondered how radiation would make me feel. I wondered what would happen to my breasts. I wondered who would take care of me. I wondered how I would make it through this. I just wanted my normal lifestyle back. I wanted to start executing the wonderful journeys that I had on my "40 while 40" agenda. I was supposed to be living my best life. Cancer was not on my list! Now, I was to begin a journey that I had not planned. There are no surprises to God, but this was a surprise to me. *Why me?* I wondered. *Why me Lord? Hadn't I already been through enough? Hadn't I already raised a child as a single mom and managed to get my son and myself through college? Hadn't life already thrown me enough curveballs?*

A couple of months after my diagnosis, I began chemotherapy. This was after a better comprehension of the road ahead and a change of doctors. After I met all those doctors, they developed a specific care plan just for me. I was given about twenty weeks of treatments but had no idea who would be available to help me. As I was told to anticipate a decline in health with each visit, I stressed over who would take me to all these appointments, as I could not drive myself. My mother and sisters worked during the day. All of this seemed well over my head.

I had always felt attending church was important. I grew up knowing God and having a relationship with Him that was ever-growing. But now I thought about Him even more. I felt alone, but I knew that He was with me. I saw what was ahead of me and could not rationalize it. I often wondered who would endure this journey with me. *God, you will have to help me with this,* I thought. I prayed that He would help me with this, and He did. God sent me some angels, who assisted with getting me to and from my appointments. These angels prayed for me and with me and supported me with household needs. My sisters and mom also provided support during my treatments. God did answer that prayer because I was no longer stressing about rides to my appointments.

My hair loss took some adjustment. Initially, I thought I would be one of the few who did not lose their hair during chemotherapy. Early in my treatment, I saw my hair was shedding some, but it seemed so little that I thought I would beat this hair loss stuff. So, I went to my hairdresser to get my hair cut and even out any breakage. She cut it low, but when she took me to the sink to wash it, my hair fell out in the sink. All of it. I was in such shock that I could not even cry. My hairdresser complimented the shape of my head, which made me feel better. I left there and made immediate plans to go to a wig shop. While all of God's creations are beautiful, I could not share my bald head with the world. It was a reminder of my current trial. I needed to embrace this new me before I could let my bald head make its reveal. I was still trying to wrap my head around what my body was going through, and I was surely not ready to take on a hair loss conversation. I never took pictures of my baldness, but in hindsight, I wish I had. Even when people see my low haircut now, they have no idea of my baldness journey.

I have a few souvenirs of my journey to remind me of what I overcame, like the scars on my chest from the surgeries and the burns from the radiation. I consider every scar and every burn a mark of triumph. I do not mind talking about the scars now, but it took me a long while to arrive here. I intended to journal my journey, but words often escaped me. So, at 40, when I thought I would be traveling the world, I stood in the mirror at my dresser looking at my bald head, asking God why

I was chosen for such a journey. While He did not answer right away, I prayed the answer would come with time.

It has been two years on this healing journey, and God has been there with me every step of the way. Even during the times, I felt alone, I knew God was near. I continued my journey to get to know Him better, especially now that I was in this trial. If I were to get through this, it would be because He allowed me. If I were to be healed, it would be because He healed me. If I were to ever be cancer-free, it would be because He did it. My relationship with Him carried me through. I was prayerful and grateful for the seeds I had planted, and if there was ever a time I needed to reap a harvest from those seeds, it was now. I needed to gather my faith in Him, in who I knew Him to be, to push through this. Together, we did.

For Your Consideration

Long before a crisis hits, we need to have an established relationship with God, be diligent students of the Word of God, and have a committed prayer life with God. So, when a crisis hits, we will be able to tap into the faith we have built up to overcome the trial we are facing because we know who our God is and what He can do. The Bible is full of relatable stories of people who were faced with trials and how they overcame them. In addition, the Bible is full of encouraging words and strategies for battle. When we are facing a crisis, the last thing we need to have to try to do is to see if God even exists. In times of crisis, we need to put our faith into action and trust everything we know about God—that He is a Healer; that He is a Provider; that He is always with us; that His Word never fails; that He will do what He says He will do; that He speaks to us; and that He hears the cries of

His children. Now is the time to revisit familiar biblical stories where we find people who overcame situations like what we are facing. Now is the time to cash in our faith chips to journey from tears to triumph.

According to the book of Matthew, a Roman officer pleaded with Jesus to heal his servant. Jesus agreed to go with him and heal the servant, but the officer, having such faith in the healing power of Jesus, said, *"Lord, I am not worthy to have you come into my home. Just say the word from where you are, and my servant will be healed"* (Matthew 8:8 NLT). The officer knew of Jesus' authority and that He need only to speak a word and it would manifest.

On the other hand, in the Old Testament, the children of Israel faced a crisis with the Egyptians pursuing them from behind, the Red Sea facing them in front, and mountains on each side. They felt trapped and feared for their lives. Instead of remembering all that God had done for them in the past and the power of God available to them in the present, they complained to God and blamed Moses. They did what we often do—they failed to pray about their circumstance to receive guidance from God, even though they had a history with God bringing them out of trial after trial. They failed to look to God in faith and succumbed to their fears. This is what happens when we forget who God is and what God has brought us through; we become overwhelmed by the trial before us. The children of Israel had Moses who told them, *"Don't be afraid. Just stand still and watch the LORD rescue you today. The Egyptians you see today will never be seen again"* (Ex. 14:13 NLT). God delivered.

Times of crisis will surely come. The people in the Bible—no matter how righteous—could not avoid them. Jesus, no matter how perfect, had them; we who are imperfect will surely have them as well. The question is how we will handle them? Will we allow our fears to drown out our faith, or will we listen to hear God's instructions to us? Will we listen to hear God's calming voice, reminding us He is with us? Will we stop and feel His presence, knowing that He said He will never leave us or forsake us? What will we do when a crisis hits?

Psalm 46:1-3 (NLV) states:

> *God is our safe place and our strength. He is always our help when we are in trouble. So we will not be afraid, even if the earth is shaken and the mountains fall into the center of the sea, and even if its waters go wild with storm and the mountains shake with its action.*

Although we know that crises will come, we are not aware of *when* they will come. If we know the Word of God, commit to a relationship with God and have a prayer life, then when the unknown comes crashing down and interrupts our plans, we are well-equipped. Even though the crisis is hard and has turned our world upside down, we know that with God we can get through it. God is our safe place. He is our strength. He is our help when in trouble. Our God is real. He will turn our tarnish into triumph.

Second Chances

JENNIFER M. SMITH

And I saw a new heaven and a new earth:
for the first heaven and the first earth were passed away.

~Revelation 21:1 (KJV)

"Sue died," said my younger brother's voice on the other end of the phone.

"Nooooooooooooooo . . . ," I screamed as I threw the phone and sobbed. Just like that, my only sister was gone. I was not ready. I knew she recently received a poor diagnosis but not much else.

In late July, four days before my sister died, a distant cousin, who shared my sister's religion and who I never met, called my brother to let us know that Sue was not doing well. We never knew she was near death. After hanging up, my brother immediately called Sue, then me. She reassured him that she was not well but expected a turnaround. He said Sue explained that she declined traditional cancer treatment but had the best naturopathic medical care. Sue said she had around-the-clock care, but she sometimes had to miss doctors' appointments because she was too weak to go.

I did not understand that Sue was near death. I saw her about six weeks earlier in mid-June, and she appeared fine. My family did not even know there was a diagnosis of anything more than a tumor that may have even been benign, but there appeared to be no urgency. I learned later that the around-the-clock care was actually hospice care with morphine to manage Sue's pain.

Maybe I was not paying attention. Maybe I did not want to accept how sick Sue was. Maybe I was upset that she had joined what I considered a religious "sect" over two decades ago, and every year she seemed to slip more away from the family and more toward the sect. Something about that group seemed to make her want to trade us for her faith. She did not want calls or texts from anyone. It hurt not to have access to her. We learned later that she did not want us to feel burdened. That broke my heart. *She is our sister*, I thought. *How could she be a burden?*

*   *   *

Sue was my first role model. She was only a year and some months older than I was, but she cared for and watched over me like she was much older. One time, she told our mother she was running away. She was four, so I was almost three. She got her red wagon and a pickle so that she could bring me with her. I sat in the wagon, eating the pickle, as we rolled up the street.

We laughed about that years later, but the memory reflected how she used to love on me.

Sue was a great sister to me. She was sensible, classy, and beautiful. She was svelte while I was often just a few pounds shy from chubby. She seemed so serious about everything when I was always playing. It was clear at a young age that she would follow in our father's footsteps as an artist. And she did.

Sue and I were sandwiched between our two brothers. The four of us were raised together with our parents in South Florida. Sue and I shared a room, so we spent most of our time together. We grew up in the 1970s when America was still working on making racial integration a reality, especially in schools. I was so close in age with Sue that it seemed we almost always attended the same schools.

A few years before Dr. Martin Luther King Jr's birthday became a national holiday in 1983, Sue asked me to help her cut out black armbands. We passed them out to interested students at our junior high school because we planned to celebrate Dr. King, even though his birthday was not yet recognized as special in America. So, we and other students—the small number of Black ones and probably a few of our white friends—tied the armbands around our upper arms in remembrance of Dr. King.

Sue was a leader whom I gladly followed. She was a natural leader, and I was her leader-in-training. In high school, she was the president of the Aristocrats, a school club serving the interests of Black students. As I recall, I was her secretary or treasurer. When Sue graduated, I ran for president and maintained many of the programs she implemented.

I really admired my sister. Sue did not see herself as I saw her. I saw this beautiful woman who exuded overwhelming confidence and who appeared to have everything together. Years later, she shared with me that she did not feel that way on the inside. Sue had lots of questions and wanted answers, like many of us.

After Sue graduated from high school, she left for college, so we no longer lived together. When I was in college and she was in graduate school, she still looked out for me. Sue would send me boxes of clothes and other things she knew I would enjoy.

When I was in my second year of graduate school, I applied for summer jobs only in Savannah so that I could spend the summer with her. By the age of 26, she already had a terminal degree (the highest academic degree that can be awarded in a particular field) and was a college dean! We had a terrific summer together for the most part. We would meet for lunch in beautiful parks. For dinner, she would grant my cuisine requests, like I was ordering from a restaurant—from red beans and rice to gumbo. On the weekends, we would hang out at the local jazz club, or go to Tybee Island to hang out on the beach. We ran together and played tennis. We would stay up and watch movies really late or talk until we fell asleep. Even though she had a guest room, I would always end up falling asleep in her bed. Although we were raised Catholic, she and I attended the historic First African Baptist Church in Savannah. I had not yet had my own religious epiphany, so I followed her to the Baptist church. Unlike the traditional Catholic church experience, we enjoyed the loud singing and praising God in the Baptist church. We did everything together. She was just phenomenal.

Sue was wonderfully accomplished, brilliant, and beautiful, but she shared that she desired things she did not have yet—marriage and maybe children. She wanted to move to South

Africa and teach because of her commitment to our African heritage. She expressed that she felt some kind of emptiness. I tried to understand, but I could not because I had not reached her level of success.

That summer, she met a man she liked. I started to notice that she no longer wanted to talk into the wee hours of the morning. She wanted me to sleep in the guest room. Something was different. It took me a while to realize that it was this guy. Because of him, I left her house two weeks before the summer ended and moved into one of those low-budget weekly rentals, but she still checked on me. To my dismay, she moved the man into her house, then married him the next summer on her birthday. Soon after, Sue resigned from her deanship. She and her husband moved to South Africa where she taught for several years.

Before she left South Africa, I noticed that she began searching for religion, or maybe peace through religion. We talked about it at some point. She wanted to memorize scripture with me that we would write on index cards, even though we were nearly 9,000 miles apart. She thought that index cards would make the scripture more accessible and digestible. I think she wanted to quiet the internal pain she felt from unhappiness. She did not just want to be married; she wanted a good husband. It was during this unfulfilling marriage that she began attending meetings of this religious sect. By the time she returned to the United States, she seemed to have formally joined that organization. When Sue and her husband moved back to the United States in early 2000, the marriage was just about over. A divorce came later. When a relative married within a year of Sue's return, she went into the church along with the other guests. But not long after when another relative died, she said her religion prevented her from going to another religion's place of worship. So, she hung around the outside but refused to enter the church for the funeral. Year after year, she went deeper into the sect.

My sister and I were no longer close like we were that Savannah summer. She seemed more guarded and defensive about her beliefs. She started leaving religious tracts around our mother's home to entice us to join her religion. None of us joined, but we also did not feel offended or insulted. The deeper she became in the religion, ultimately becoming a minister, the more distant she became with the family. She would forgo activities with us to go door-to-door to spread the word about the religion with her church members. Whenever Sue came to a new town, she would find church members and cultivate friendships with them. Little by little, she drifted away from us. She still never seemed content or at peace, but she was busy. The religion kept her busy, and her social life eventually was mainly with the members.

A year before her death, Sue called. "Hey, I am attending my church's conference in Orlando and wanted to stay with you."

"Sure," I said. I was taking care of our father. He would be at the house with us. That week, a hurricane was set to come through my town. The conference was canceled. She hung out with Dad and me for the week. We had an absolute ball! It was just like we were in Savannah—before she met her ex-husband. We watched movies in my room until the wee hours. We biked on the tandem bike around the neighborhood and to the movies. We went out to eat several times, even with some of my friends. She made me delicious avocado rolls. We walked the local bike trail. We painted together. We floated in the pool for hours, talking about all sorts of things. It was just like old times. We really enjoyed each other.

What was different, though, was that we did not really share meaningful things. Maybe we were becoming reacquainted with one another. I am not sure. Maybe she wanted to talk about religion. Sue did share that she was a minister in hers, but I did not reveal that I was in mine. Maybe I was afraid that our religious differences would cause conflict. I am not sure. We did not discuss deep topics like we once had done. I was incredibly happy that she seemed to want to do things with me again. I just embraced the moment.

Later that year in November, my stepfather passed. Sue placed her house on the Savannah market and moved to our mother's home to help Mom. During that time, Sue's breathing became increasingly compromised, almost simultaneously with the spread of the coronavirus. She went for testing. All her COVID-19 tests were negative. A scan revealed some issues in the lungs, but not how devastating they were. A tumor was identified, but none of us knew much more.

In mid-June while I was visiting Mom and Sue, Sue moved about two hours away from our mother's home to be closer to her doctors. I had a chance to say a quick goodbye to Sue. I expected to see her again soon. She moved into an in-law suite owned by a member of the religious sect. Our family had little access to Sue after that. Mom would call and text. Sometimes Sue would respond. Evidently, she was gravely ill, but no one alerted us.

In late July, my brother received a call. Sue was very ill, but we were not informed of how severe or what the illness was. We had no idea that she was on the brink of death or that metastatic lung cancer cells were ravaging her body. We knew she wanted no calls and no texts. She gave us an address to write her, but nothing more. I wanted to at least text her, but I also wanted to honor her wishes, so I did not call or text. I copied the address, intending to write soon.

Soon never came. Death beat it.

*   *   *

Just before dawn in early August, the phone ring awakened me. My brother called to tell me that Sue died. We had no details. Information was slim. After I threw the phone, I sobbed. By now, I was on the carpet. My chest heaved as I struggled to catch my breath.

"You promised to heal her!" I accused God. "You didn't! You didn't even tell me she was that sick! I can't trust You!"

I pounded my hand on the carpet. I thought about Sue and how much I would miss her. But I also thought about all the years that I allowed our relationship to be shallow and almost non-existent. Was I really angry at God or myself?

Next, I attacked Sue. I yelled in the air at her.

"How dare you! How dare you shut us out when you needed us! We were always there for you! Why were you okay with a religion that alienated you from your family? We could have helped you get the medical attention you needed!" I screamed at the top of my lungs. "You didn't have to die!"

I believed that she was tired of advocating for her health, and I knew our family could have intervened effortlessly to help her if we had access to her.

I learned later that she wanted desperately to be healed, but she was also tired. And that is what she told our mother at some point, "I'm tired, Mom."

Was she in pain? I wondered. *Was someone with her? Did she ask for us? Had we departed on good terms? Was I good to her? Did I tell her I loved her enough? Did she know I loved her? Why didn't God save her?*

Honestly, I felt betrayed . . . by someone or something . . . I was not sure. I was not ready. I was not ready for her to die. I did not know that I would never see or talk to her again after she had left our mother's house that day in June. But sometimes, we are not allowed more than the chance we have today. Are we ever ready? *She was too young, but others much younger have died*, I thought. I should have been grateful for the more than half a century God loaned her to us. For the moment, that was not enough.

All of a sudden, I felt my knees stinging. I am not sure when that morning, but somehow, I managed to rub the top layer of skin off both knees from the carpet. I stepped in the shower and let the water run on hot for nearly an hour. My knees stung even more. My tears and the water stream blended. When I exited the shower, I could see my neck and upper chest were virtually lobster red. I dressed to go buy coffee and sat in my driveway with that coffee for about an hour, never drinking even a sip. I had already spoken to our family. I learned a few days after Sue died that our mother intended to do a surprise visit and show up on Sue's doorstep two days after Sue died. Death beat Mom's visit too. But Mom saw Sue once more.

But what now? I wondered. I stared straight ahead at the garage door. I noticed everything about it, from the color to the cobwebs. I told my employer I was taking leave for the next few months, then retracted it later that day. I pondered life, and no one seemed more important than my sister. I wondered if she knew how much we loved her. *How come she wanted to be around those people more than her family?* I wondered. Maybe when she wanted to share with me how she felt and why she was drawn to this religion, I was not listening. Maybe I made her feel small for wanting to be a part of that. I could have allowed her to share about her religion. I could have shared more about mine. I could have figured out what was more similar in our beliefs than focusing on what I thought was different.

I received a text the day she died that she was going to be cremated. The funeral was already set up without any real involvement from our family. I learned from the distant cousin that he had spent 26 years working in the sect's headquarters. Before that, he started studying to become a Catholic priest. He said that the sect, too, believes that Jesus is Lord and Savior. The sect's members consider themselves Christians. He expressed exasperation with the various rumors about his religion. I told him that his beliefs seemed to contradict my research; however, I was happy to hear that he, and I imagine my sister also, believes that Jesus is Lord and Savior and that I thought it remained from his and Sue's Catholic upbringing. I later explained to him that the sect's secrecy surrounding Sue's illness and surrounding the unconscionable seizure of her personal belongings left me skeptical. Scenario after scenario went through my mind as to the possibilities of how Sue could still be alive today, but it was all fruitless. I hoped and believed that the brothers and sisters in her sect offered her some sense of community, comfort, and care in her last days.

Today was a lesson—there is no guarantee about tomorrow, I thought. "But I already knew that, so how come today had to be a lesson?" I questioned myself out loud.

I *knew* the lesson but did not live it. While Sue was living, I went on as though I could always apologize and get a second chance. All the times I thought that I could have engaged my sister in conversation but did not.

I lay on my bed. I ignored the texts and calls because by now most of the family's friends knew that Sue had died. I apologized to God. I was mad at myself, not Him, but I needed a target this morning. I was not mad at Sue either.

I lay in silence. The light in my room was dim. I heard what sounded like a squirrel crawling up the screen of my sliding glass door.

Never again, I thought, *will I hear my sister's voice. Never again will I see her smile at me. Never again will we ride the tandem bike together. Never again will we laugh at the stupid things on TV. Never again will we watch movies until the wee hours in the morning. Never again will we float in the pool together. Never again . . .*

I wanted a do-over. I thought about all the things I would do if God gave me a second chance with Sue. I would listen to her. I would try to understand her. I would tell her my deep secrets again. I would talk about religion with her and listen to her heart. I would tell her I loved her every time we hung up the phone as she often did. I would hug her every time I saw her. I would love her hard . . . harder than I did the first go-round . . . if God gave me a second chance . . . .

Why didn't God give me a second chance with Sue? I wondered. Oh, but He did. The God of Second Chances did. The many times I saw her, He gave me a second chance to love her harder than the last. The many times I texted her, He gave me a do-over. The many times I spoke to her, He gave me another opportunity. Every single time, I had another opportunity—a second chance. But I often blew it. Thinking I had more time with her allowed me to miss each second chance. Thinking I could apologize later for my thoughtless texts or comments allowed me to miss another second chance.

Yeah, I thought as I lay there, *I'm not mad at God or Sue; I'm mad at myself.*

I learned that Sue died at about 12:30 a.m. Central Time, 1:30 a.m. on the East Coast. *Wow, I woke up at 1:30 a.m.,* I thought. I lay in bed, alert. So, God did awaken me. I should have prayed like I often do when He awakens me in the wee hours. Normally, I search my heart for who God may have dropped in my Spirit, then pray for them, but not that morning. Instead, I just lay there wondering why I was awake, then fell back asleep until my brother's call at 5:21 a.m.

A few hours later, I reached for my phone and searched it to find the pictures that Sue and I took when she spent a week at my house a year ago. I studied our faces, our smiles. We were smiling from deep within—nothing was fake. I loved her hard that week. She loved me back, just as hard. She was the best sister for me; God made sure of that. God gave me more than a second chance with her. He gave me so many with Sue. I just neglected to use them all. Now, they were all gone. Now, I only had memories of the second chances God gave me. I posted the best of the pictures from her last visit with me on social media: "See you again, sis. R.I.H."

I told our dad, who has a spotty memory, that MJ died this morning. He has good and bad days. Today seemed to be a good day.

"What happened? Why did she die?" Dad asked. "Was she sick?" He was so compassionate in his questions. His face looked so kind and concerned.

"She was sick, Dad. Maybe tumors but not really sure."

He was silent. Then, he said, "I will pray for her lots." He paused again. Then, he asked, "Will she go to heaven?"

"Yes," I said. "She will be in heaven."

"How do you know?" he questioned.

"Because she was a good person," I responded.

He smiled. "Me too?" he inquired.

"Yes, you too Dad. And me too, I hope."

I know. Folk will say, "Being good is not the test." But I was speaking to our elderly father in a delicate state of mind. God will judge, not us. Plus, it is too hard to think of anything else. God is a kind and loving God—at least mine is. I have never been a "fire and brimstone" believer. I am not sure of all that Sue believed, but we could pray together. She and I both ended with "In Jesus' name, Amen." I learned later that near the time of her death with labored breathing surrounded by those in the sect, she was led into prayer that I imagined closed with "In Jesus' name, Amen."

Today's lesson was hard, but I learned it, I think. Today is a second chance for something. To be better today than I was to others yesterday. To be more loving than yesterday. To see everyone and miss no one—strangers and friends. To show the best version of me because today is my second chance.

*　　*　　*

Exactly two months after Sue died, Mom saw Sue. Mom said she was awake, or so she thought, when she saw Sue with a huge smile on her face.

"Sue, what do you want?" Mom asked.

Sue did not respond, but she was still smiling with a gigantic smile. Mom thought about waking me as I was sleeping next to her but decided against it. Mom closed her eyes and went to sleep with so much peace about Sue. That was the last time any of us saw her.

I was leaving to go back home that day after spending a few weeks with Mom. Sue's last visit gave Mom and me so much peace. We knew that Sue was okay, and I also knew that Mom was going to be okay too.

For Your Consideration

Sometimes, we have lots of time to say goodbye. Other times, we have no chance. In those instances, we feel like we are not ready. Even when we are not ready, God is. When we feel like we have wasted precious time with unimportant matters and lost unrecoverable moments thinking that we would see or hear our loved ones again, He knows. When tragedy strikes, many of us wish we had more time to plan, as though we could re-write the end of the story. He knows.

We want a do-over. A second chance. A new start. A fresh beginning. A new chapter. A clean slate. Another day. Another minute. Another second. *Wait*, we think. *One more chance, Lord.* But time waits for no one.

We may not have a second chance with a particular person, experience, or issue, but God is a God of Second Chances. We will be afforded a do-over. Our deceased loved ones are gone, but there are chances with others whom we love and others who are alive.

In the book of Luke, Jesus is on the cross between two criminals. One asks Jesus to remember him in the eternal kingdom. Jesus obliged, then promised the criminal a second chance. Jesus replied, "*Today shalt thou be with me in paradise*" (Luke 23:43 KJV).

We must receive the lesson and move forward. To ponder what we would have done had God let us know that we would never see a loved one again is useless. Those lessons are hard.

Those lessons are painful. Those lessons are ones we do not forget. Those lessons should soften our hearts toward others. Those lessons should make us re-evaluate our lives and what is important. *Did we get a lesson today? Did we already know the lesson but were not living it? Are we now living the lesson?*

Today, God has given us a second chance for something meaningful—to tell a loved one something special—to do something kind for a stranger—to spend time with someone who needs a shoulder to lean on. Today, the sun has risen once again. The rising sun is a sign from the Risen Son that we have a second chance to do and be better than yesterday.

Do not delay. Uplift someone today. Encourage someone today. Congratulate someone today. Apologize to someone today. Forgive someone today. Minister to someone today. Help someone today. Use today wisely. God has given us a do-over. Today, we have a second chance.

Prayer of Salvation

God, thank You for sending Your only son, Jesus, to die on the cross for my sins. Thank You, Jesus, for shedding Your blood in order for me to be redeemed from the curse of sin. Please forgive me for everything that I have done that does not please You. Forgive me for my thoughts that have kept me separated from You. Come into my life. Save me. Change me. Deliver me. Set me free. I receive You as my Savior and my Lord. Help me to live right. I make this confession with my mouth, that Jesus is Lord, and I believe in my heart that God raised Jesus from the dead, according to Romans 10:9-10. Because of this, I am saved. I am a new creature. Old things are passed away, and all things in my life are brand new. In Jesus' name, I pray, Amen.

We receive salvation by grace through faith. It is a gift from God. There is nothing you can do to earn it or deserve it. It is absolutely free.

To help you in your new walk:

- Tell an encouraging friend, family member, or co-worker about your new commitment to serve Jesus.

- Talk to the Lord every day! Ask Him to fill you with the Holy Spirit. Ask the Lord to help you keep your eyes on Him. Communication is a critical key to any relationship. You do not have to use fancy words or sit in any special position. Just pray.
- Find a Bible-believing church where you can be planted so that you can grow in your new walk.
- Read the Bible every day.
- Learn the basics of Christianity.

Prayer for Hard Times and Endurance

Heavenly Father, I come before You, acknowledging that You are the Almighty God. I repent of any sin that has separated me from You. Cleanse my heart and turn Your ear to hear my cry. You are more than enough to meet my needs. You carried the children of Israel through many difficult seasons, and You caused them to endure. You brought them out of danger and bondage with Your powerful hand.

Now, I need You to guide me in this difficult season. I am feeling overwhelmed by the situations around me. I am feeling intimidated by the challenges and obstacles in front of me. I do not know which way to turn. I feel as if my back is against the wall. I feel abandoned and alone in this battle. The natural forces working against me are robbing me of my joy and my peace. But I know that greater are You that is in me, than he that is in the world. Help me, God.

The battle against me is intense. I declare that the battle is not mine, but it belongs to You, and that no weapon formed against me shall prosper. I need You to intervene right now. Make the crooked places in my life straight. Make the rough places in my life smooth. Cancel every attack from the enemy, against my life, against my mind, against my family, against my finances, against my health, against my faith, and against my future. Cause insufficiency to leave me now. You are my God, and You shall supply all of my needs according to Your riches in glory by Christ Jesus.

I need Your help to keep from quitting. Please reassure me that You are with me. Let me feel Your presence. Show me Your hand of favor and blessing. Help me to stand still and wait to see Your deliverance.

When I feel a profound sense of loneliness, when I feel entangled in a deep pit of depression and despondency, when loneliness has devoured my joy and overtaken my life, and when I can see no way out of this dark and lonely ditch, remind me of Your goodness. Your Word promises that You are all I need and that You will never leave me. Pull me out of the pit of pain and pessimism. Help me to feel the warmth of Your love. Satisfy my deepest longings with Your presence.

You promise to heal the brokenhearted. Help me to believe and receive this. Comfort my heart and bring peace to my mind. Help me to be patient with the process that I am walking through. Strengthen my faith and do a new thing in me. Let Your will be done in every area of my life. Close every door that needs to be closed. Open every door that I need to access. Shift my thinking to a higher level. Help me to develop a posture of expectation and an abundance mentality. Help me to take the limits off my life. Catapult me through every glass ceiling and beyond every barrier that has been imposed by others and myself.

Lord, remember me as You did for Abraham, Hannah, Rachel, Noah, and so many others in the Bible. You never forget Your people or Your promises. I continue to cry out to You with prayer and petition, with praise and thanksgiving.

By Your grace, I am stepping out of this unproductive space into a dimension of creativity and productivity. I will not fail. I will not quit. I will not grow weary. I will trust You with my whole heart. I will praise instead of complaining. I will count my blessings. I will encourage others. I will take my thoughts captive and change my thinking as well as my behavior. I will dwell on Your Word and hide it in my heart. I will allow You to direct my paths. Draw me into Your presence, by Your power, and for Your glory. In Jesus' name, I pray, Amen.

Daily Prayer

Thank You, God, for another day. Thank You for extending new mercy toward me. Thank You for allowing Your grace to rest on me. Thank You for watching over me and everything that concerns me. I repent of any sin in my life. Cleanse my hands and my heart. Renew a right spirit within me.

Walk with me today. Order my steps and my stops. Help me to walk in Your ways. Give me wisdom for every decision. Silence the voice of the enemy that tries to confuse and distract me. Make Your will clear to me. Help me to guard my heart for out of it proceeds the issues of life. Protect and stabilize my thoughts. Help me to think on things that are true, just, honest, pure, lovely, of good report, and things that have virtue and praise. Cancel every depressing thought and every heavy spirit that tries to weigh me down.

Help me to be aware of the negative influences in my life. Help me to walk in discernment. Help me to know when advice given to me is ungodly. Lord, keep my feet from straying and keep me from falling. Help me to avoid people and things that waste my time and rob me of momentum.

Help me to lead with godly influence and compassion. Help me to see others through Your eyes so that I may love as You love. Help me to be as concerned about others as I am about myself.

I renounce pride and every dark and evil spirit that tries to contaminate my spirit. Liberate my life from every chain of bondage, every generational curse, and every cultural stronghold. Set me free from self-imposed limitations and help me to soar past limitations imposed by others. Take the lid off my life. Give me the courage and the charisma to boldly access spaces and arenas that I and others have previously been denied access to. Help me to take the perils from my past and use them as steppingstones into my future. Help me to focus on the plans that You have for me. You know the thoughts You think concerning me. They are thoughts of peace and not evil, to give me hope and a future. Help me to remember that Your thoughts and ways are higher than mine. I trade my plans for Your purpose.

"Many are the plans in the mind of a man, but it is the purpose of the Lord that will stand" (Proverbs 19:21 ESV). In all that I do today, help me to honor You by allowing my light to shine that all may see my good works and glorify You. In Jesus' name, I pray, Amen.

Connect with Us!

Facebook: Official Agape Perfecting Praise &
Worship Center; Sharon Y. Riley
Ministries

Email: agapeppwc@aol.com

Web Address: www.agapeppwc.com

Mail: Agapé Perfecting Praise &
Worship Center
P.O. Box 618421
Orlando, FL 32861
(407)293-6264